**ASSOCIATE & LICENTIATE DIPLOMA
SYLLABUS 1999 EDITION
Effective 1 September 1998**

This Syllabus replaces all previous diploma syllabi of both
Western Ontario Conservatory of Music and The Western Board of Music,
and will remain in effect until further notice.

This Syllabus contains requirements for

Associate Diploma (Performer) for PIANO, VOICE, PIPE ORGAN, GUITAR

Associate Diploma (Teacher) for PIANO, VOICE

Licentiate Diploma (Performer) for PIANO, VOICE, PIPE ORGAN

Please contact the Conservatory Office for requirements for instruments not included in this Syllabus

The Conservatory expresses appreciation for advice and proof reading to Lisa Barkey, Clark Bryan,
Tammy-Jo Mortensen, Kevin Love, and Anita Ruthig

Third Printing
10 November 1999

Welcome to

CONSERVATORY CANADA

The two founding institutions of Conservatory Canada bring the past and the future together, creating a new, nation-wide organization out of two eminent regional institutes.

Western Ontario Conservatory of Music in London, Ontario was established in 1891 and incorporated in 1934. Throughout the years it has maintained a teaching facility, and began offering province-wide examinations in the late 1930's. This was later expanded to serve Atlantic Canada.

Music teachers and university administrators in the provinces of Alberta, Saskatchewan and Manitoba formed The Joint Board of Music for Western Canada in 1934. Soon re-named The Western Board of Music, it developed a comprehensive examination system to serve the three Prairie provinces, and in recent decades expanded into British Columbia.

In September 1997, both Western Ontario Conservatory and The Western Board merged to create Conservatory Canada. Based at Western Ontario Conservatory's music building in London, Conservatory Canada maintains a western regional office in Edmonton, the former Western Board location.

Within and outside the regular examination system, each founding institution has sought to provide teachers and students with varied, innovative programs and features. Oral questions, supplementary pieces, mini-lessons, recital assessments and teacher development assessments have all been carried over into the new syllabi and program offerings of Conservatory Canada.

Previous credits earned with either Western Ontario Conservatory or The Western Board are automatically retained, and are now portable throughout Canada. Production and revision of syllabi, repertoire books and other support materials is an ongoing process, with the New Millennium Series of repertoire books in both piano (pre-grade 1 to grade 10) and voice (grade 1 to grade 8) to be released in June 1999.

Conservatory Canada offers the best of two worlds, the new and the old: a new national vision for the 21st century, steeped in the traditions of two venerable Canadian examination systems. We welcome the opportunity to serve Canadian musicians, both young and old, amateur and professional, from coast to coast.

Contents

I. GENERAL INFORMATION

Conservatory Canada awards professional diplomas of *Associate in Music* and *Licentiate in Music*.

ASSOCIATE DIPLOMA

The Associate Diploma is offered in Performance and in Teaching in the following practical areas.

In **Performance** for

Piano	Voice	Violin
Organ	Guitar	Viola
Trumpet	Flute	Cello
French Horn	Clarinet	

In **Teaching** (Pedagogy) for

Piano	Voice	Violin

The Associate Diploma is NOT offered in the areas of Theory or History.

LICENTIATE DIPLOMA

The Licentiate Diploma is offered in Performance only in the following practical areas:

In Performance ONLY for

Piano	Voice	Violin
Organ	Guitar	Viola
Trumpet	Flute	Cello
French Horn	Clarinet	

The Licentiate Diploma is NOT offered in the areas of Theory or History or Teaching (pedagogy).

1. SESSIONS

a) Practical Examinations

The Conservatory conducts two practical examination sessions during each academic year. These examinations include most instruments and voice, and are held at centres throughout Canada (new centres may be established by arrangement with the Conservatory):

1. WINTER SESSION-	last two weeks in February
	(application deadline is normally early December)
2. SPRING SESSION-	the entire month of June
	(application deadline is normally early April)

Applicants should consult the current examination form for the deadline date of the specific session for which they wish to apply.

The Conservatory will make every effort to schedule examinations around legitimate events, such as school trips or school examinations, provided notice is given IN WRITING AT THE TIME OF APPLICATION. However, because of constraints in reserving facilities and Examiners, **this cannot be guaranteed, and by submitting an application, the candidate agrees to appear for the examination as scheduled.** Candidates entering the June examinations must understand that it is not always possible to schedule music examinations around school examinations.

Candidates will be given at least two-weeks notice of the date, time and place of the practical examination. Under no circumstances are Diploma candidates or their teachers permitted to change dates or times of the scheduled examination. Examiners are instructed not to make schedule changes unless such changes have been authorized by the Office of the Registrar.

b) Written Examinations
The Conservatory conducts three written examination sessions during each academic year throughout Canada (new centres may be established by arrangement with the Conservatory):

1. WINTER SESSION-	second Saturday in January	(application deadline is normally mid-November)
2. SPRING SESSION-	second Saturday in May	(application deadline is normally early March)
3. SUMMER SESSION	third Saturday in August	(application deadline is normally early July)

Applicants should consult the current examination form for the deadline date for the specific session for which they wish to apply, and for the date and exact time of day for the examination.

2. APPLICATIONS
All applications must be made using the current application form. Completed forms must be submitted in person, or by mail, courier, or fax (using Visa or Mastercard) to:

> The Office of the Registrar
> Conservatory Canada
> 45 King Street, Suite 61
> London, Ontario, N6A 1D0
> Fax: 519-433-7404
> Email: officeadmin@conservatorycanada.ca

Application forms are available from any of the Conservatory's regional offices, and from local music stores.

A separate application form is required for each examination. All applications must be completed neatly and accurately; applications lacking necessary information may be subject to a surcharge, or rejected. Applications must be accompanied by the correct fees and must be received by the Office of the Registrar in London, Ontario NO LATER THAN THE CLOSING DATE. Applications arriving after the deadline date will be rejected and returned, *regardless of the postmark date*.

Each partial or supplemental examination requires a new application, and partial examinations should be clearly, marked as *1st part* or *2nd part*.

3. CENTRES
Practical examinations are conducted by fully qualified Examiners appointed by the Conservatory in those centres where the number of applicants is deemed sufficient. The Conservatory reserves the right to defer examinations until a later session in any centre where the enrollment does not warrant the visit of an Examiner, or to require the candidate to travel to the nearest viable centre. The best facilities

available will be provided for examinations, in centres as close as possible to the candidate's hometown. Candidates should plan to arrive at least 15 minutes before the examination is scheduled to begin.

4. PAYMENT OF FEES

The appropriate fee must be included with the completed application form. A current fee schedule appears on the application form each year. Fees may be paid by cheque, Visa or Master Card. DO NOT SEND CASH THROUGH THE MAIL. Applications submitted by fax must use either Visa or Master Card.

5. APPEALS

Queries or appeals concerning the examination procedure must be filed in writing with the Office of the Registrar within 10 days of the completion of the examination.

6. CANCELLATIONS

Notice of withdrawal, for any reason, must be submitted in writing to the Office of the Registrar. Consult the current application form for refund policy regarding cancellations by the candidate before the scheduled date of the examination. No refund will be considered for notice of cancellation, for whatever reason, received after the scheduled date of the examination.

7. MARKING STANDARDS

The Conservatory's standard of marking, in Diploma examinations is as follows:

First-Class Honours with Distinction	90-100 marks
First-Class Honours	80-89 marks
Honours	70-79 marks
Insufficient to Pass	Below 70 marks

8. CONDITIONAL STATUS & SUPPLEMENTARY EXAMINATIONS.

Candidates for the *Teacher* diploma who obtain an over-all pass mark, but who fail to obtain the minimum mark required in one or more sections of the Practical examination will be placed on *Condition*, and will be permitted to take a Supplemental examination in that section(s) of the examination that is *Conditioned*. All sections receiving a *Conditioned* status must be completed successfully within a period of twelve months immediately following the date of the original examination. Candidates who fail to complete fully the requirements within this period must re-enter for the complete examination.

Applications for Supplemental Examinations should be submitted in the usual way, observing the normal application deadlines.

Candidates for the *Performer* diploma who obtain an over-all pass mark, but who fail to obtain the minimum mark required in one or more sections of the Practical examination, are NOT eligible for Conditional Status and Supplementary Examinations and will be required to repeat the entire examination.

9. RESULTS AND NOTICES

All examination notices, results and certificates are normally sent to the teacher for distribution to the candidates, unless specifically requested otherwise at the time of application. Under no condition will examination results be released verbally, either in person or by telephone. Because examination marks are confidential to the teacher and candidate, results CANNOT be released to any other person.

10. MEDAL FOR EXCELLENCE

A Medal for Excellence will be awarded in each academic year to the candidate for the Associate (Performer) and the Associate (Teacher) diplomas who receives the highest average mark of all required practical and co-requisite subjects for the respective instrument or voice.

To be eligible a candidate must:

i) have a minimum over-all average grade of 80%, with a minimum grade of 70% in each required co-requisite course. A maximum of TWO required theory and/or history courses may be transferred credits, but in this case the marks originally received for these courses will NOT be used to compute the over-all average.

ii) complete in ONE sitting the Conservatory Canada Associate practical examination. Candidates who take partial or supplemental examinations are NOT eligible for medals.

Both professional and amateur musicians are eligible for the Associate Medals for Excellence.

11. AWARDING OF DIPLOMAS

Candidates who have satisfied all prerequisite and corequisite requirements are eligible to be awarded the diploma at the annual Convocation of the Conservatory, normally held in early November of each year. Only those candidates who have been awarded the *Associate* diploma at Convocation are entitled to announce themselves as an Associate of Conservatory Canada and to use the initials

A.C.C.M. (Performer) or **A.C.C.M. (Teacher)**

Only those candidates who have been awarded the *Licentiate* diploma at Convocation are entitled to announce themselves a Licentiate of Conservatory Canada and to use the initials

L.C.C.M.

12. ACADEMIC DRESS

Conservatory Canada academic dress is

Associate

Black gown and mortarboard cap of black felt with black tassel. An Aberdeen-shaped hood of black silk, fully lined with teal green, and with a two-inch border of pink taffeta on the anterior edge of both sides.

Licentiate

Black gown and mortarboard cap of black felt with black tassel. An Aberdeen-shaped hood of black silk, fully lined with teal green, and with a two-inch border of pink taffeta on the outside anterior edge and of white taffeta on the inside anterior edge.

II. REGULATIONS FOR PRACTICAL EXAMINATIONS

1. CONDUCT OF PRACTICAL EXAMINATIONS

i) Only the Examiner, or Examiners, and the candidate will be permitted to be present in the examination room during the progress of the examination. Where piano accompanists are needed, they will be permitted in the room only for those portions for which their services are required.

ii) Recording equipment is not permitted in the examination room.

iii) In accordance with copyright law, photocopies of musical scores (for use by the candidate or accompanist or the examiner) are NOT permitted in the examination room unless the candidate can present written authorization from the copyright holder. The examiner has been instructed NOT to proceed with the examination while unauthorized photocopies are present.

iv) Candidates must list in the appropriate place on the back of the examination notice all repertoire to be performed in the examination. This list must be given to the examiner at the start of the examination.

2. EDITIONS

Any standard edition of the music may be used for the examination. However, candidates are encouraged to choose editions that represent the composer's intentions in the clearest, and most straightforward manner. Candidates may NOT use simplified or adapted versions of works to be performed.

3. PARTIAL EXAMINATIONS

i) Partial examinations (where the examination is divided into two equal parts and taken at two different sessions) are available only for the Practical examination for the Associate *Teacher* diploma. Partial examinations are NOT permitted for Associate *Performer* or *Licentiate* candidates. *Associate (Teacher)* candidates who opt for a partial examination must include the Viva Voce and the performance of the pre-Associate Grade pieces (Grades 3-10 as required) at the same sitting. The first part must contain **no less than 44% and no more than 56%** of the requirements.

ii) The division of the examination is left to the discretion of the candidate. Sections given a composite mark (*e.g.* the complete technical requirements or the complete aural tests) may not be sub-divided and must be completed at one sitting. At each sitting the list presented to the Examiner must contain details of all components that are to be heard. Each section as it is presented will be awarded a mark.

iii) No portion of a partial examination completed during the first sitting may be repeated at the second sitting in an attempt to improve the mark already awarded.

iv) The total mark at the conclusion of the second sitting determines the standing of the candidate. There is no recourse to an adjustment of this final mark for any reason. If the result of the first sitting is low, then it might be to the candidate's advantage to start over.

v) The appropriate examination fee must be paid with the first application. A new application must be submitted for the second sitting, for which an additional fee is charged.

vi) The second part of a partial examination must be completed within twelve months following the first sitting, and must include all aspects not previously examined.

vii) Candidates who choose to play a partial examination will not be eligible for the Medal for Excellence.

ASSOCIATE DIPLOMA GENERAL REGULATIONS

I. REQUIRED COURSES

To be awarded the Associate Diploma, all candidates must complete successfully each of the following Pre-requisite courses AND Co-requisite courses.

A. Required Pre-requisite Courses		B. Co-requisite Courses	
History 5	A survey course covering the period from the early Christian era to approximately 1800.	**Practical Instrument/Voice**	A practical examination in the candidate's principal instrument. Specific requirements will vary for the Performer and the Teacher diplomas. Completion of Grade 10 practical examination is NOT a pre-requisite.
History 6	A survey course covering the period from approximately 1800 to the present day.	**History 7**	An in-depth study of a specific historical period chosen by the candidate.
Theory 6	The combined study of harmony, basic counterpoint, and simple forms.	**Theory 7 (A)**	The combined study of chromatic harmony, invertible counterpoint and fugue.
Functional Piano	Required for all instruments other than keyboard and guitar. Candidates who have completed successfully Grade 6 Piano are not required to take the Functional Piano Examination.	**Theory 7 (B)**	The study and analysis of standard musical forms and structures.
		Pedagogy 7 (Teacher Candidate's only)	A written examination on pedagogical principles, methods, techniques and repertoire as they relate to the candidate's principal instrument.

Requirements for all Theory and History courses may be found in Conservatory Canada's Theory & History Syllabus (1999 edition). In addition, requirements for all Theory 7(A), Theory 7(B), History 7 and Pedogogy 7 co-requisite courses are also included in this Diploma Syllabus.

II. TRANSFER CREDITS

Transfer credit is not possible for practical subjects. However, candidates who have completed successfully equivalent examinations in Theory and History courses at recognized conservatories and/or universities may apply in writing for consideration for transfer credit. If approved, the transfer credit can be used to satisfy the co-requisite requirement for the awarding of a practical certificate. The following regulations will apply:

1) To apply for a transcript evaluation with a view to obtaining transfer credit, candidates must

   i) submit a letter of application, with the appropriate fee, to the Office of the Registrar. Include:
      a) a list of courses completed for which transfer credit is being sought, and

b) a copy of the appropriate course descriptions from the Calendar/Syllabus in effect when the examination was taken.

ii) arrange to have an official transcript (or letter) sent by the issuing institution **directly** to the Office of the Registrar. No application for transfer credit will be considered until the official transcript is received. Transcripts sent by the candidate are NOT acceptable.

2) Transfer credit will NOT be considered for pre-requisite courses completed more than TEN years before the scheduled date of the practical examination session, nor for co-requisite courses completed more than FIVE years before the scheduled date of the practical examination session.

3) Transfer credit will NOT be given for either Pedagogy 7 or the Practical examination (or any portion thereof).

IV. REGULATIONS FOR THE ASSOCIATE PRACTICAL EXAMINATIONS

1. AGE LIMIT
Candidates for the Associate *Teacher* diploma must have reached eighteen years of age before they can register for the Practical examination. There is no age restriction on the Associate *Performer* Diploma.

2. TIME LIMIT
i) ALL pre-requisite courses must be completed, or transfer credit approved, **before the registration deadline** for the session at which the candidate wishes to register for the Practical Examination.

ii) Required History, Theory and Pedagogy (if required) co-requisite courses not completed successfully before the Practical examination must be completed within FIVE years of the initial practical examination. If all courses are not completed successfully within this period, then the candidate will be required to retake the practical examination.

3. PARTIAL EXAMINATIONS
i) *Performer:* The practical examination must be completed in one 60-minute session.

ii) *Teacher:* The practical examination may be completed in either one 2-hour session, or over two examination sessions of approximately 55 minutes each. *(For specific details and regulations concerning Partial Examinations, Please see above, clause II.3.)*

4. CHOICE OF PIECES
You may choose your entire repertoire for the examination from

i) the *List Pieces* given in this Syllabus. Please contact the Conservatory for List Pieces for other instrument not included in this Syllabus.

OR

ii) your own choice of pieces not included in this Syllabus (or in the Syllabus for Grades 1 - 10) but which are of equivalent difficulty and meet the List categories found under the Practical Requirements for your instrument. These own choice pieces will be considered as Irregular List Pieces.

OR

iii) any combination of Syllabus List Pieces and own choice pieces.

PLEASE NOTE that all own-choice (*i.e. Irregular List*) pieces require the approval of the Conservatory. Requests for approval must be made in writing and must be received at the Office of the Registrar at least 30 days before the application deadline for the examination session. In choosing your examination repertoire, the following will apply:

i) The use of obbligato instruments and/or ensemble music such as duets and trios are not permitted. Solo concerto movements are NOT permitted for Piano, though they may be used for other solo instruments.

ii) Substitution is not permitted for the teaching repertoire in the *Teacher* Examination.

iii) In choosing the examination program, candidates are advised to consider appropriate level of difficulty, and over-all artistic balance. They should also ensure that the entire program is not longer than 60 minutes of music.

5. PRINTED SCORES & EDITIONS

i) Any standard edition of the music may be used for the examination. However, candidates are encouraged to choose editions that represent the composer's intentions in the clearest, and most straightforward manner.

ii) The candidate must provide the examiner with original printed copies of ALL works to be performed. Photocopies are NOT acceptable.

6. MEMORIZATION

For the *Performer* diploma, ALL pieces and technical requirements must be performed from memory. For the *Teacher* diploma, only Technical Requirements must be performed from memory, except for Voice in which the Associate pieces must also be memorized.

7. TECHNICAL TESTS EXEMPTION

For the *Performer* diploma only, candidates who have completed successfully the Grade 10 Practical examination using the syllabus requirements of Conservatory Canada or Western Ontario Conservatory of Music or The Western Board, will not be required to be examined in those areas listed below in which they obtained a minimum grade of 70% in Grade 10:

> Technical Tests (including Vocalizes for singers)
> Keyboard Skills (if required)
> Sight Reading
> Aural Tests

This exemption is only applicable if the Grade 10 examination was completed no more than 10 years before the scheduled date of the Associate practical examination. This exemption does NOT apply to Organ candidates.

8. PERFORMANCE OF PIECES

The examiner will hear ALL pieces without interruption.
No repeats (other than da capo) are to be performed.

**Candidates are expected to know all of the current regulations and requirements
for the examinations as outlined in this Syllabus. No allowance can be made
for candidates who misread or fail to follow any of the regulations and/or
requirements for the examination.**

V. REGULATIONS FOR THE LICENTIATE PRACTICAL EXAMINATIONS

1. PRE-REQUISITE

In order to proceed to the Licentiate examination, candidates must hold the *Associate (Performer) Diploma* from any one of Conservatory Canada, The Western Board of Music, or Western Ontario Conservatory of Music. Candidates who hold an Associate Diploma awarded by other institutions may apply in writing to the Registrar, *at least six months in advance of the date of the examination application deadline*, for special permission to proceed to the Conservatory Canada Licentiate examination. However, such permission is not automatic and is considered on a case by case basis.

2. TIME LIMIT

There is no limit on the time between the completion of the Associate (Performer) Diploma and the Licentiate examination.

3. EXAMINATION CENTRES

Licentiate Diploma examinations are given only at London, Edmonton and other selected centres. Please contact the Conservatory for the Licentiate examination centre nearest you.

4. CONDUCT OF THE EXAMINATION

A jury of TWO examiners will conduct the examination.

The examiners will hear ALL pieces without interruption. No repeats (other than da capo) are to be performed.

5. PARTIAL EXAMINATIONS

Partial examinations are not possible, and the Licentiate practical examination must be completed in one sitting.

6. PRINTED SCORES & EDITIONS

i) Any standard edition of the music may be used for the examination. However, candidates are encouraged to choose editions that represent the composer's intentions in the clearest, and most straightforward manner.

ii) The candidate must provide the examiners with original printed copies of ALL works to be performed. Photocopies are NOT acceptable.

7. MEMORIZATION

ALL pieces must be performed from memory (except for organ).

**Candidates are expected to know all of the current regulations and requirements
for the examinations as outlined in this Syllabus. No allowance can be made
for candidates who misread or fail to follow any of the regulations and/or
requirements for the examination.**

ASSOCIATE
Piano (Performer)

Length of Examination: 75 minutes

Examination Fee: Please consult the current examination application form for the schedule of fees.

Co-requisites: Successful completion of THREE written examinations is required for the awarding of the Associate (Performer) Diploma, as follows:
Theory 7(A), Theory 7(B), History 7

Marking

Section	Requirement	Total Mark Possible	Minimum Mark Required
A	SIX LIST PIECES To be performed from memory, one from each of		
	List A (Baroque)	17	11
	List B (Classical)	17	11
	List C (Romantic)	17	11
	List D (Impressionist or Early 20th century)	17	11
	List E (Late 20th century, not Canadian)	16	10.4
	List F (Canadian composition)	16	10.4
B	TECHNICAL TESTS Scales Triad/Chords Arpeggios	Pass/Fail	Pass
	KEYBOARD SKILLS Harmonization Transposition	Pass/Fail	Pass
	SIGHT READING Rhythm Pattern Piano Passage	Pass/Fail	Pass
	AURAL TESTS	Pass/Fail	Pass
	MEMORY (included in marks for List Pieces)		–
C	OVER-ALL TOTAL	100%	70%

Candidates must obtain:

a) A minimum mark in **each** of the List pieces as specified under Section A.

b) A "Pass" in each section of the Technical Tests & Musicianship Skills as listed under Section B. A candidate will be exempt from these tests in any section(s) in which he/she received the minimum mark in the Grade 10 Conservatory Canada examination. (See Regulation IV. 7 given above.)

c) A minimum over-all average mark of 70%.

Candidates who fail to obtain the minimum grade in one or more of the requirements listed above (under a, b, or c) shall be required to repeat the ENTIRE EXAMINATION at a subsequent session.

REQUIREMENTS

A) Pieces

Candidates must be prepared to play SIX pieces, at least one of which must be a Prelude or Toccata or Fantasia and Fugue (or similar) and one of which must be a complete sonata of at least three movements. Pieces must be chosen as follows:

        One from List A (Baroque Period)
        One from List B (Classical Period)
        One from List C (Romantic Period)
        One from List D (Impressionist Period or early 20th century)
        One from List E (modern, not Canadian)
        One from List F (by a Canadian Composer)

Pieces should be chosen to contrast in style, key, tempo, mood, etc. Your choice must include six different composers. All pieces must be performed from memory. No mark will be awarded for any piece where the musical score is used.

Pieces may be chosen from the Lists or candidates may choose their own repertoire from pieces not included in this Syllabus but of equal difficulty to those given in the Lists. Pieces that appear in Lists for previous Grades *(Piano Syllabus, 1999 edition)* may not be used. Candidates are reminded that own-choice pieces are classified as *Irregular List Pieces* and must be submitted to the Office of the Registrar for approval in accordance with Regulation IV.4 given above.

B) Technical & Musicianship Tests

All technical tests must be played from memory, evenly, with good tone, and logical fingering. Metronome markings should be regarded as *minimum* speeds.

KEYS REQUIRED

	New Keys	Review Keys
Major	None	ALL KEYS
Minor	None	ALL KEYS

Technique

SCALES

To be played ascending AND descending, in the keys stated.

	Keys	*Hands*	*Octaves*	*M.M.* $\downarrow=$	*Articulation*
Major (separated by 8ve)	ALL keys	together	4	126	legato and staccato in sixteenth notes
Harmonic minor (separated by 8ve)	ALL keys	together	4	126	legato and staccato in sixteenth notes
Melodic Minor (separated by 8ve)	ALL keys	together	4	126	legato and staccato in sixteenth notes

Separated by 3rd (tonic in left hand)	E, F	together	4	126	legato in sixteenth notes
Separated by 6th (tonic in right hand)	E, F	together	4	126	legato in sixteenth notes
Octaves	ALL keys	together	2	84	solid staccato in sixteenth notes
Double 3rds	B♭, E♭, D♭	together	2	60	legato in sixteenth notes
Contrary motion	ALL major keys ALL minor (harm.) keys	together	2	126	legato in sixteenth notes
Chromatic octaves	beginning on any note	together	2	84	solid staccato in sixteenth notes

CHORDS

To be played ascending AND descending, in the keys stated.

	Keys	Position	Hands	Octaves	M.M. ♩ =	Note Values
Solid 4-note Chords (Major & Minor)	ALL Keys	Root & Inversions	together	2	120	in quarter notes
Solid Chords (Dominant 7th)	of ALL Keys	Root & Inversions	together	2	120	in quarter notes
Solid Chords (Diminished 7th)	of ALL Keys	Root & Inversions	together	2	120	in quarter notes
Broken 4-note Chords (Major & Minor)	ALL Keys	Root & Inversions	together	2	120	in sixteenth notes
Broken Chords (Dominant 7th)	of ALL Major Keys	Root & Inversions	together	2	120	in sixteenth notes
Broken Chords (Diminished 7th)	of ALL minor Keys	Root & Inversions	together	2	120	in sixteenth notes
Broken Alternating Patterns	A, B, D♭ g#, f, b♭	Root & Inversions	together	2	120	in sixteenth notes

ARPEGGIOS

To be played ascending AND descending, in the keys stated.

	Keys	Position	Hands	Octaves	M.M. ♩ =	Note Values
Arpeggios (Major & Minor)	ALL Keys	Root & Inversions	together	4	96	in sixteenth notes
Arpeggios (Dominant 7th)	ALL Major Keys	Root & Inversions	together	4	96	in sixteenth notes
Arpeggios (Diminished 7th)	ALL minor Keys	Root & Inversions	together	4	96	in sixteenth notes

NOTE: ARPEGGIOS: Candidates must play all positions in sequence (e.g. the full arpeggio in root position, followed by the full arpeggio in first inversion, and followed similarly in second inversion, and, for 7th chords, in third inversion). Candidates may be asked to begin the sequence starting with the arpeggio in either root position or in ANY inversion.

PIANO (Performer)

Keyboard Skills

Progressions	Harmonization	Transposition
NONE	To harmonize a melody at sight, ending with a Perfect or Plagal Cadence, as appropriate. ◆Chords I, IV and V, root and 1st inversion required. (ii and vi chords may be used but not required.) ◆Keys: up to and including 4 sharps or flats ◆No indication for chord changes will be given. ◆V7 chords may be used but are not required. ◆Moving bass and passing notes required.	To transpose a simple two-voice passage of music at sight. ◆Up or down a tone or semi-tone. ◆To or from any key with no more than 4 sharps or flats. ◆Difficulty: about Grade 3

Example: Harmonization

Sight Reading

Candidates are required to perform at sight a) a rhythmic exercise and b) a passage of piano score as described below. The candidate will be given a brief period to scan the score, but not to "practise silently" before beginning to play. Candidates must perform each section without counting aloud. It is recommended that candidates maintain a steady beat, and avoid the unnecessary repetition caused by attempting to correct errors during the performance.

Rhythm	Piano Passage
To tap, clap or play on one note (at the candidate's choice) a rhythm in simple or compound time. May include syncopated rhythms, changing-meters, irregular meters, and complex patterns. Length 4-8 bars Time signature any simple or compound time Note values variety of values including ties Rest values variety of values	To play at sight a short piece equal in difficulty to pieces of Grade 6-7 level, in any style or period. May include modulations, changing meters and irregular meters Keys Major & Minor ALL keys Length 16-32 bars

Example: a) Rhythm

Aural Tests

Candidates will be required:

i)   at the candidate's choice, to play back OR sing back to any vowel, the **lower** part of a two-part phrase in a major key, after the Examiner has:
       ✓named the key [up to and including three sharps or flats]
       ✓played the 4-note chord on the tonic in solid form
       ✓played the passage twice.

PIANO (Performer)

The parts may begin on ANY note of the tonic chord. Following is the approximate level of difficulty:

ii)   to identify any of the following intervals after the Examiner has played each one once. Intervals may be
played   in melodic (broken) form OR harmonic (solid) form.

ABOVE a note	BELOW a note
major and minor 2nd	*major and minor 2nd*
major and minor 3rd	*major and minor 3rd*
perfect 4th	*perfect 4th*
augmented 4th (diminished 5th)	*augmented 4th (diminished 5th)*
perfect 5th	*perfect 5th*
major and minor 6th	*major and minor 6th*
major and minor 7th	*major and minor 7th*
perfect octave	*perfect octave*

iii)   to identify any of the following 4-note chords after each has been played once by the Examiner.

major and *minor* chords: root position and first or second inversion [to be played in solid form, close position]
dominant 7th chords: root position or any inversion [to be played in solid form, close position]
diminished 7th chords: root position only [to be played in solid form, open (SATB) position]

iv)   to state whether a short piece in *chorale* style is in a *major* or a *minor* key, and whether the final cadence and
all internal cadences are *Perfect* (V-I), *Imperfect* (I-V, II-V, IV-V), *Plagal* (IV-I), or *Interrupted/Deceptive*
(V-VI). The Examiner will play the passage TWICE; the first time straight through without interruption, the
second time stopping at cadence points for the candidate to identify them.

ASSOCIATE
Piano (Teacher)

Length of Examination: 115 minutes

Examination Fee: Please consult the current examination application form for the schedule of fees.

Co-requisites: Successful completion of FOUR written examinations is required for the awarding of the Associate (Teacher) Diploma, as follows:
Theory 7(A),   Theory 7(B),   History 7,   Pedagogy 7

Marking

Section	Requirement	Total Mark Possible	Minimum Mark Required
A	THREE ASSOCIATE LIST PIECES One from each of 1. A Complete Prelude & Fugue or Sonata 2. ONE Piece from List C or List D 3. ONE Piece from List F (Canadian) TOTAL MARK FOR THIS SECTION	 8 8 8 24	 15.6
	TWENTY-ONE PIECES Chosen from Grades 3-10 Repertoire Lists Grades 3-7 Grades 8-9 Grade 10 (List E) TOTAL MARK FOR THIS SECTION	 8 8 7 23	 15.0
B	TECHNICAL TESTS Scales Triad/Chords Arpeggios	10	6.5
	KEYBOARD SKILLS Harmonization Transposition	9	5.9
	SIGHT READING Rhythm Pattern Piano Passage	6	3.9
	AURAL TESTS	8	5.2
C	VIVA VOCE	20	13
D	OVER-ALL TOTAL	100%	70%

Candidates must obtain:

a) The total minimum mark in each of the Associate List pieces and the Graded Repertoire pieces as specified under Section A.

b) The minimum mark in each of Technical Tests, Keyboard Skills, Sight Reading, and Aural Tests as listed under Section B.

c) The minimum mark in Viva Voce as specified under Section C.

d) A minimum over-all average mark of 70%.

Candidates who fail to achieve the required minimum mark in any section(s) (A, B, or C) will be given conditional status in that section and must complete successfully a Supplemental Examination in the conditioned section(s) within twelve months of the original examination. Candidates who fail to achieve the required minimum over-all average mark of 70% will not be eligible for supplemental examinations and will be required to repeat the ENTIRE EXAMINATION at a subsequent session.

REQUIREMENTS

A) Pieces

Candidates must be prepared to perform a total of TWENTY-FOUR pieces chosen as follows:

I) THREE Associate level pieces, chosen as follows:

    1) *Either* ONE complete Prelude & Fugue from the Baroque Period (List A)
    or ONE complete sonata from the Classical Period (List B)

    2) ONE piece chosen from either the Romantic Period (List C) or the Impressionist Period/early 20th century (List D)

    3) ONE piece by a Canadian composer (List F)

II) TWENTY-ONE pieces from Grade 3 through Grade 10 repertoire Lists of Conservatory Canada Piano Syllabus (1999 edition).

Candidates must be familiar with Conservatory Canada's piano repertoire books, the New Millennium Series, and at least ten of the twenty-one pieces must be chosen from this series. *(This regulation comes into effect beginning with the February 2000 session and following. It is NOT in effect for the February 1999 and June 1999 examination sessions.)*

Pieces must be chosen as follows:

    1) ONE piece from Grade 10, List E

    2) FOUR pieces from Grades 8 and 9 repertoire, chosen as follows:

        ONE from List A (must be either a two-part or a three-part Invention by J. S. Bach),
        ANY ONE from List B
        ANY ONE from List C
        ANY ONE from List D
        Pieces must be chosen to include two pieces from Grade 8 and two pieces from Grade 9.

    3) SIXTEEN pieces from Grades 3 to 7 repertoire, chosen as follows:

        THREE pieces from Grade 3:   One each from List A, List B, and List C
        THREE pieces from Grade 4:   One each from List A, List B, and List C
        THREE pieces from Grade 5:   One each from List A, List B, and List C
        THREE pieces from Grade 6:   One each from List A, List B, and List C
        FOUR pieces from Grade 7:   One each from, List A, List B, List C, and List D

    The choices should comprise a well-balanced program of contrasting styles, keys, moods, tempo and types. The selections should also represent a variety of composers.

NOTE: Candidates must present to the Examiner a complete list of the twenty-one pieces prepared; however, the examiner may not necessarily hear every work on the list.

B) Technical & Musicianship Tests

All technical tests must be played from memory, evenly, with good tone, and logical fingering. Metronome markings should be regarded as *minimum* speeds.

KEYS REQUIRED

Major	ALL KEYS
Minor	ALL KEYS

Technique

SCALES
To be played ascending AND descending, in the keys stated.

	Keys	Hands	Octaves	M.M. ♩=	Articulation
Major (separated by 8ve)	ALL keys	together	4/3	132	legato in sixteenth notes (4 octaves) AND staccato in triplet eighth notes (3 octaves)
Harmonic minor (separated by 8ve)	ALL keys	together	4/3	132	legato in sixteenth notes (4 octaves) AND staccato in triplet eighth notes (3 octaves)
Melodic Minor (separated by 8ve)	ALL keys	together	4/3	132	legato in sixteenth notes (4 octaves) AND staccato in triplet eighth notes (3 octaves)
Separated by 3rd (tonic in left hand)	ALL keys (Major only)	together	4	132	legato in sixteenth notes (4 octaves)
Separated by 6th (tonic in right hand)	ALL keys (Major only)	together	4	132	legato in sixteenth notes (4 octaves)
Octaves	ALL keys (Major & Minor)	together	2	88	solid staccato in sixteenth notes
Double 3rds	ALL keys (Major only)	together	2	60	legato in sixteenth notes
Contrary motion	ALL major keys ALL minor (harm.) keys	together	2	132	legato in sixteenth notes
Chromatic Double Octaves	beginning on any note	together	2	92	solid staccato in sixteenth notes

CHORDS

To be played ascending AND descending, in the keys stated.

	Keys	Position	Hands	Octaves	M.M. ♩ =	Note Values
Solid 4-note Chords (Major & Minor)	ALL Keys	Root & Inversions	together	2	126	in quarter notes
Solid Chords (Dominant 7th)	of ALL Major Keys	Root & Inversions	together	2	126	in quarter notes
Solid Chords (Diminished 7th)	of ALL minor Keys	Root & Inversions	together	2	126	in quarter notes
Broken 4-note Chords (Major & Minor)	ALL Keys	Root & Inversions	together	2	126	in sixteenth notes
Broken Chords (Dominant 7th)	of ALL Major Keys	Root & Inversions	together	2	126	in sixteenth notes
Broken Chords (Diminished 7th)	of ALL minor Keys	Root & Inversions	together	2	126	in sixteenth notes
Alternating Patterns	All Keys	Root & Inversions	together	2	120	in sixteenth notes

ARPEGGIOS

To be played ascending AND descending, in the keys stated.

	Keys	Position	Hands	Octaves	M.M. ♩ =	Note Values
Arpeggios (Major & Minor)	ALL Keys	Root & Inversions	together	4	104	legato in sixteenth notes
Arpeggios (Dominant 7th)	ALL Major Keys	Root & Inversions	together	4	104	legato in sixteenth notes
Arpeggios (Diminished 7th)	ALL minor Keys	Root & Inversions	together	4	104	legato in sixteenth notes

NOTE: ARPEGGIOS: Candidates must play all positions in sequence (e.g. the full arpeggio in root position, followed by the full arpeggio in first inversion, and followed similarly in second inversion, and, for 7th chords, in third inversion.) Candidates may be asked to begin the sequence starting with the arpeggio in either root position or in ANY inversion.

Keyboard Skills

Harmonization	Transposition
To harmonize a melody at sight, ending with a Perfect or Plagal Cadence, as appropriate. ◆Chords primary and secondary chords with inversions required. ◆Keys: up to and including 4 sharps or flats ◆No indication for chord changes will be given. ◆Use V7 and ii7 chords. ◆Employ interesting accompaniment patterns with moving bass and passing notes.	To transpose a simple piano passage at sight. ◆Up or down a tone or semi-tone. ◆To or from any key (major and minor) with no more than 4 sharps or flats. ◆Difficulty: about Grade 4

PIANO (Teacher)

Sight Reading

Candidates are required to perform at sight a) a rhythmic exercise and b) a passage of piano score as described below. The candidate will be given a brief period to scan the score, but not to "practise silently" before beginning to play. Candidates must perform each section without counting aloud. It is recommended that candidates maintain a steady beat, and avoid the unnecessary repetition caused by attempting to correct errors during the performance.

Rhythm	*Piano Passage*
To tap, clap or play on one note (at the candidate's choice) a rhythm in simple, compound or irregular time. May include syncopated rhythms, changing-meters, irregular meters, and complex patterns.	To play at sight a short piece equal in difficulty to pieces of Grade 7-8 level, in any style or period. May include modulations, changing meters and irregular meters
Length 4-8 bars	Keys ALL keys (Major & Minor)
Time Signature any simple or compound time	Length 16-32 bars
Note values variety of values including ties	
Rest values variety of values	

Example: a) Rhythm

Aural Tests

i) At the candidate's choice, to play back **on the piano** both parts of a two-part phrase (approximately four bars) in either a major or a minor key, after the examiner has named the key, given the tonic chord, and played the passage twice.

Example:

ii) Identify melodic intervals after each has been played once (either ascending or descending). All major, minor, and perfect intervals, and also augmented 4th and major or minor 9th.

iii) Identify time signatures of short passages of music after each has been played once.

iv) Identify, by symbols, chord progressions in root position only employed in a four-bar phrase, in major key only, beginning on the tonic. Chords on the I, ii, IV, V, vi, and vii°$_6$, and a cadential 6/4 may be used. The examiner will play the tonic chord and then will play the entire phrase twice. During the second playing the examiner will stop after each chord for the candidate to identify the harmony.

C) Viva Voce

1) Candidates are required to demonstrate a knowledge of methods of teaching including:

   a) the first lesson;

   b) practising methods, technical routine, aural training, sight reading, memorization;

   c) the mechanism of the piano and the function of the pedals;

   d) the position and action of the fingers, hand, wrist and arms and the relation of each to tone production and development of facility and control;

   e) the teaching of technique, keyboard harmony, and transposition;

   f) stylistic interpretation and other musical matters in general.

2) Candidates should have a strong practical acquaintance with a variety of beginner's books (for both the young and mature beginner), teaching material, repertoire for more advanced levels, technical exercises both for examination requirements (i.e. scales, chords, arpeggios, etc.) and for non-examination purposes (i.e. for solving specific technical difficulties presented by the repertoire, etc.).

3) Candidates must be prepared to demonstrate the teaching of any piece from those List pieces (Grades 3 - 10) as presented by the candidate for performance in the practical portion of this examination:

   a) to show how the piece should be introduced to the student;

   b) to recognize any special difficulties in the piece and to demonstrate how each might be overcome;

   c) to demonstrate the teaching of the notation, time, rhythm, tone, dynamics, interpretation, style and form of the piece;

   d) a demonstration lesson of one piece chosen by the examiner. The examiner may perform the piece, introducing certain errors, and the candidate will be expected to detect such errors and to demonstrate how to correct them.

4) The candidate should have a secure and broad knowledge of musical style and interpretation as applied to piano literature, including dynamics, phrasing, articulation, tempo, rhythm, ornamentation, etc.

5) The candidate must display a basic knowledge of Canadian composers and compositions.

LIST A
Baroque Period

BACH, J.S.
English Suites
 No. 2 in A minor, BWV 807
  (Prelude, Sarabande, AND Gigue)
 No. 4 in F major, BWV 809
  (Prelude, Sarabande AND Gigue)
 No. 5 in E minor, BWV 810
  (Prelude, Allemande AND Sarabande)
 No. 6 in D minor, BWV 811
  (Prelude, Courante AND Sarabande)
French Suites, BWV 812–817
 Any ONE Complete
Partitas
 No. 1 in B flat major, BWV 825
  (Allemande, Sarabande, AND Gigue)
 No. 2 in C minor, BWV 826
  (Sinfonia, Allemande AND Sarabande)
 No. 4 in D major, BWV 828
  (Allemande, Sarabande, AND Gigue)
 No. 5 in G major, BWV 829
  (Prelude, Allemande AND Sarabande)
 Sonata in D major, BWV 963
  (Complete)
 Suite in A minor, BWV 818
  (Complete)
Toccatas
 Any ONE
Well-tempered Clavier, Vol. 1
 Prelude & Fugue No. 1, BWV 846
 Prelude & Fugue No. 3, BWV 848
 Prelude & Fugue No. 4, BWV 849
 Prelude & Fugue No. 7, BWV 852
 Prelude & Fugue No. 8, BWV 853
 Prelude & Fugue No. 12, BWV 857
 Prelude & Fugue No. 15, BWV 860
 Prelude & Fugue No. 19, BWV 864
 Prelude & Fugue No. 20, BWV 865
 Prelude & Fugue No. 22, BWV 867
 Prelude & Fugue No. 24, BWV 869
Well-tempered Clavier, Vol. 2
 Prelude & Fugue No. 4, BWV 873
 Prelude & Fugue No. 5, BWV 874
 Prelude & Fugue No. 11, BWV 880
 Prelude & Fugue No. 13, BWV 882
 Prelude & Fugue No. 14, BWV 883
 Prelude & Fugue No. 16, BWV 885
 Prelude & Fugue No. 17, BWV 886
 Prelude & Fugue No. 18, BWV 887
 Prelude & Fugue No. 21, BWV 890
 Prelude & Fugue No. 22, BWV 981
 Prelude & Fugue No. 23, BWV 892
FISCHER, J.K.T
Musicalische Parnassus
 Suite No. 5 (Erato) (Complete)
HÄNDEL, G.F.
 Suite No. 4 in E minor
  (EITHER Fugue & Gigue
  OR Allemande, Sarabande & Gigue)

Suite No. 8 in F minor
 (EITHER Prelude & Fugue
 OR Allemande, Courante & Gigue)

LIST B
Classical Period

BEETHOVEN, L. van
11 New Bagatelles Op. 119
 (Complete)
6 Bagatelles Op. 126 (Complete)
Sonatas
 any ONE Complete, *except*:
 Op. 27, No 2 (Grade 8)
 Op. 49, No. 1 or 2 (Grade 8)
 Op. 27, No. 1 (Grade 9)
 Op.79 (Grade 9)
 Op. 2 No. 1 (Grade 10)
 Op. 10, No. 1, 2, or 3 (Grade 10)
 Op. 13 (Grade 10)
 Op. 14, No. 1 or 2 (Grade 10)
 Op. 28 (Grade 10)
 Op. 78 (Grade 10)
 Op. 90 (Grade 10)
Variations
 15 Variations and Fugue on an original theme, Op. 35 ("Eroica
  Variations")
 33 Variations on a waltz by Diabelli, Op. 120
CLEMENTI, M.
 Sonata in B minor Op. 40 No. 2
HAYDN, F.J.
 Andante con Variazione in F minor, Hob. XVII:6
Sonatas
 A flat major, Hob.XVI:46
 E flat major, Hob.XVI:49
 C major (The English),Hob.XVI:50
MOZART, W.A.
Sonatas
 D major, K. 284
 C major, K. 309
 A minor, K. 310
 D major, K. 311
 B flat major, K. 333
 C minor, K. 457
 F major, K. 533 (Complete)
 D major, K. 576
Variations
 10 Variations on *Unser dummer Pobel meint* by Gluck, KV 455

LIST C
Romantic Period

BRAHMS, J.
Ballades
 Op. 10 No. 2 OR 3
Capriccios
 Op. 76, Nos. 1, 2, 5, 8 (any ONE)
 Op. 116, Nos. 1, 3, 7 (any ONE)

PIANO (Repertoire)

Intermezzi
Op. 116, No. 4
Op. 118, No. 6
Rhapsodies
Op. 79, No. 1 OR 2
Op. 119, No. 4
Scherzo, Op. 4
Sonatas
Op. 1 (1st movement)
Op. 2 (1st movement)
Op. 5 (1st movement)
CHOPIN, F.
Ballades
Choose ANY ONE of
Op. 23 in G minor
Op. 38 in F
Op. 47 in A flat
Op. 52 in F minor
Berceuse Op. 57
Etudes
Op. 10
Choose ANY ONE
Op. 25
Choose ANY ONE, except No. 2
Fantaisie-Impromptu, Op. 66
Impromptu, Op. 36
Nocturnes
Op. 27,
Choose ANY ONE of
Nos. 1, 2
Op. 37, No. 2
Op. 48, No. 1
Op. 62, No. 1
Polonaises
Op. 26, No. 2
Op. 44
Preludes
Op. 28,
Choose ANY FOUR of
Nos. 1, 8, 12, 14, 16, 17, 18, 19, 23, 24
Scherzos
Op. 20 in B minor
Op. 31 in B flat minor
Op. 39 in C sharp minor
Op. 54 in E major
Waltz, Op. 42
FAURÉ, G.
Barcarolles
Op. 41, No. 2
Op. 42, No. 3
Op. 66 No. 5
Op. 70, No. 6
Impromptus
Op. 31, No. 2
Op. 34, No. 3
Op. 102, No. 5
Nocturnes
Op. 33, No. 1
Op. 33, No. 2
Op. 37, No. 5
Op. 63, No. 6
Op. 74, No. 7
Op. 107, No. 12
Op. 119, No. 13
GRIEG, E.
Sonata, Op. 7

LIADOV, A.
Arabesque in A major, Op. 4, No. 2 *(A Liadov Album)*
LISZT, F.
Waldesrauschen OR Gnomenreigen
Années de Pèlerinage, Book 1
No. 4, Au bord d'une source
Années de Pèlerinage, Book 2
Choose ANY ONE of
No. 5 Sonetto 104 del Petrarca
No. 6 Sonetto 123 del Petrarca
Années de Pèlerinage, Book 3
No. 4 Les jeux d'eaux à la Villa d'Este
Ballade in B minor
Hungarian Rhapsodies
Choose ANY ONE of
Nos. 6, 8, 10, 11, 13, 15 (any ONE)
Polonaise in E major
Trois Etudes de Concert
Choose ANY ONE of
No. 2 in F minor (La Leggierezza)
No. 3 in D flat (Un Sospiro)
6 Paganini Etudes
Choose ANY ONE
12 Transcendental Etudes
Choose ANY ONE
MENDELSSOHN, F.
Andante and Rondo Capriccioso, Op. 14
6 Preludes and Fugues Op. 35
Choose ANY ONE of
No. 2 in D
No. 3 in B minor
No. 4 in A flat
No. 5 in F minor
No. 6 in B flat
Etude in F minor
Fantasy in F sharp minor, Op. 28
Variations in E flat, Op. 82
Three Etudes Op. 104(a)
Choose ANY ONE
SCHUBERT, F.
Sonatas
Choose ANY ONE of
A minor, Op. 164 D. 537
A, Op. 120 D. 664
A minor, Op. 143 D. 784
Impromptus
Op. 90, D. 899
Choose ANY ONE of
No. 1 in C minor OR
No. 3 in G flat
Op. 142 D. 935
No. 1 F minor
SCHUMANN, R.
Etudes on Caprices of Paganini, Op. 10
Choose ANY ONE of
Nos. 2, 3
Etudes Symphoniques, Op. 13
Theme AND Choose ANY SIX variations
Fantasiestücke, Op. 12
Choose ANY ONE of
No. 5 In der Nacht
Faschingsschwank aus Wien, Op. 26
First OR Last movement
Novelletten, Op. 21
Choose ANY ONE of
Nos. 2, 8

Papillons Op. 2 (Complete)
Scenes from Childhood, Op. 15
  Choose ANY EIGHT
Variations on the name ABEGG, Op.1

LIST D
Impressionist & Early 20th Century

ALBENIZ, I.
Iberia Suite
  Choose ANY ONE of
    No. 1 Evocacion
    No. 2 El Puerto
Suite Espagnole, Op. 232
  Choose ANY TWO of
    No. 3 Sevilla
    No. 5 Asturias-Leyenda
    No. 6 Aragon
    No. 7 Castilla
DEBUSSY, C.
Ballade
Danse
Estampes
  Choose ANY ONE of
    No. 1 Pagodes
    No. 2 La Soirée dans Grenade
    No. 3 Jardins sous la pluie
Etudes, Book I
  Choose ANY ONE of
    Nos. 1, 6
Etudes, Book II
  Choose ANY ONE of
    Nos. 1, 6
Images, Book 1
  No. 1 Reflets dans l'eau
  No. 2 Hommage à Rameau
  No. 3 Mouvement
Images, Book 2
  Choose ANY ONE of
    No. 1 Cloches à travers les feuilles
    No. 2 Et la lune descend sur le temple
    No. 3 Poissons d'or
Préludes, Book 1
  Choose ANY ONE of
    No. 3 Le Vent dans la plaine
    No. 5 Les Collines d'Anacapri
    No. 7 Ce qu'a vu le vent d'ouest
    No. 10 La Cathédrale engloutie
    No. 11 La Danse de Puck
Préludes, Book 2
  Choose ANY ONE of
    No. 3 La Puerta del vino
    No. 4 Les Fées sont d'exquises
    No. 7 La terrasse des audiences du clair de lune
    No. 8 Ondine
    No. 12 Feux d'artifice
Suite pour le Piano (1901)
  Choose ANY ONE of
    Prélude
    Toccata

DOHNANYI, E. von
Rhapsodies, Op. 11
  Choose ANY ONE of
    No. 2 in F sharp minor
    No. 3 in C
6 Concert Etudes, Op. 28
  Choose ANY ONE of
    Nos. 5, 6
GERSHWIN, G.
3 Preludes (Complete)
Gershwin at the Keyboard
  Liza
GRANADOS, E.
Goyescas
  Choose ANY ONE movement
GRIFFES, C.
Fantasy Pieces, Op. 6
  Choose ANY ONE
IRELAND, J.
Island Spell
POULENC, F.
Deux Novellettes
  No. 2
Improvisations
  Choose ANY THREE
Intermezzo (1943) in A flat
Presto in B flat
Suite Française (Complete)
Toccata
RACHMANINOFF, S.
Etudes Tableaux, Op. 33
  Choose ANY ONE, except No. 8
Etudes Tableaux, Op. 39
  Choose ANY ONE
Moments Musicaux
  Op. 16
    Choose ANY ONE, except No. 3 or No. 5
Preludes, Op. 23
  Choose ANY ONE of
    Nos. 2, 5, 6, 7
Preludes, Op. 32
  Choose ANY ONE of
    Nos. 3, 5, 9, 10, 12
RAVEL, M.
Valses nobles et sentimentales
Miroirs
  Choose ANY ONE
  Noctuelles
  La Vallée des cloches
Jeux d'Eau
Le Tombeau de Couperin
  No. 6 Toccata
SCRIABIN, A.
12 Etudes, Op. 8
  Choose ANY ONE of
    Nos. 8, 9, 10, 12
8 Etudes, Op. 42
  Choose ANY ONE of
    Nos. 1, 5, 6, 7, or 8 (any ONE)
Etude, Op. 49, No. 1
Etude, Op. 56, No. 4
Three Etudes Op. 65
  Choose ANY ONE
SMETANA, B.
3 Polkas Op.7
  No. 1 in F sharp major

6 Bohemian Dances
Bohemian Dance in A minor - Presto
TOCH, E.
Burlesken Op. 31
No. 3 The Juggler

LIST E
Modern (Not Canadian)

BARBER, S.
Excursions
Choose ANY TWO
Ballade, Op. 46
Nocturne, Op. 33
BARTOK, B.
Allegro Barbaro
3 Burlesques, Op. 8C (Complete)
2 Elegies, Op. 8B
No. 1
Mikrokosmos, Vol. VI
No. 144 Minor seconds,
Major Sevenths
AND No. 146 Ostinato
Out of Doors Suite
Choose ANY ONE
Rumanian Christmas Songs
EITHER Series 1 (Complete)
OR Series 2 (Complete)
2 Rumanian Dances Op. 8A
Choose ANY ONE of
Nos. 1, 2
3 Studies Op. 18
Choose ANY ONE
BERGSMA, W.
3 Fantasies (Complete)
BERNSTEIN, L.
4 Anniversaries (Complete)
CARROLL, G.
Elegy
COPLAND, A.
Passacaglia
Piano Sonata (any ONE movement)
DUBOIS, P.M.
Etudes de Concert
Choose ANY ONE
FERGUSON, H.
5 Bagatelles, Op. 9 (Complete)
FINNEY, R.L.
Variations on a Theme by Alban Berg
FISHER, A.
6 Aphorisms (Complete)
GINASTERA, A.
Malambo
Suite de danzas criollas
Choose ANY THREE
GODOWSKY, L.
53 Studies on Chopin Etudes
Choose ANY ONE

HARRIS, R.
Toccata
HINDEMITH, P.
Ludus Tonalis
Interludium & Fuga in E
Sonata No. 2 (Complete)
HONEGGER, A.
Prelude, Ariosos et Fughetta sur le nom de BACH
7 Pièces Brèves (Complete)
Trois Pieces
Hommage à Ravel *AND* Danse
KABALEVSKY, D.
Sonata in F, No. 3 (Complete)
24 Preludes Op. 38
Choose ANY ONE of
Nos. 3, 6, 10, 14, 16
Spring Games and Dances, Op. 81
KHACHATURIAN, A.
Toccata
MARTIN, F.
8 Preludes for Piano
Choose ANY TWO contrasting
MENOTTI, G.C.
Ricercare *AND* Toccata
MESSIAEN, O.
Preludes pour Piano
Choose ANY ONE of
No. 2 Chant d'extase
No. 4 Le nombre Léger
No. 8 Un reflet dans le vent
MUCZYNSKI, R.
Masques
PROKOFIEV, S.
4 Etudes, Op. 2
Choose ANY ONE
4 Pieces Op. 4
No. 4 Suggestion diabolique
10 Pieces Op. 12
No. 10 Scherzo
Toccata, Op. 11
Visions Fugitives Op. 22
Choose ANY FOUR
Sonata No. 1, Op. 1 (Complete)
Sonata No. 3, Op 28 (Complete)
2 Sonatinas, Op. 54
No. 1 in E minor
RAWSTHORNE, A.
Bagatelles
SCHÖNBERG, A.
Drei Klavierstücke, Op. 11
Choose ANY ONE
Zwei Klavierstücke Op. 33a
SESSIONS, R.
From My Diary
Choose ANY ONE of
Nos. 2, 4
SHOSTAKOVICH, D.
24 Preludes and Fugues Op. 87
Choose ANY ONE *except:*
No. 2 or No. 5 (Grade 10)
WEBERN, A.
Variations Op. 27

LIST F
Canadian Composers

ADASKIN, M.
Sonata for Piano (Complete)
BECKWITH, J.
Etudes
Choose ANY TWO
BEHRENS, J.
Feast of Life
CARDY, P.
The Masks of Astarte
CHAMPAGNE, C.
Quadrilha Brasileira
CHERNEY, B.
Danse Crepuscule du Souvenir
Choose ANY TWO
COULTHARD, J.
4 Etudes (1945)
Choose ANY ONE
Free Variations on the name BACH
Sonata for Piano, 1947-48 (First movement only)
Aegian Sketches (Complete)
Image astrale
Image terrestre
CRAWLEY, C.
Aubade
Twelve Preludes for Piano
Choose ANY EIGHT
ECKHARDT-GRAMATTÉ, S.
From My Childhood, Vol. II
Etude de concert
EVANGELISTA, J.
Monodías Españolas
Choose ANY EIGHT
HETU, J.
Prelude et Danse
Variations
INHALT, I.
Fantasia
JAQUE, R.
Suite pour Piano No. 2 (Complete)
Etude et fantasie
KENINS, T.
Sonata (Complete)
KYMLICKA, M.
5 Preludes (Complete)
Sonatina No. 1 (Complete)

MORAWETZ, O.
Scherzo
Suite for Piano
Dance
MOREL, F.
Deux etudes de sonorité
No. 2
PAPINEAU-COUTURE, J.
Etude en Si^b
Suite for Piano
Rondo
PENTLAND, B.
Toccata
Studies in Line (Complete)
PEPIN, C.
Suite pour piano
Choose ANY ONE Movement
PREVOST, A.
Improvisation
ROGERS, W.K.
6 Short Preludes on a Tone Row (Complete)
ROSEN, R.
Set II
Choose ANY TWO
SAINT-MARCOUX, M.C.
Mandala II
SCHNEIDER, E.
Homage to S.R. (Sergei Rachmaninoff)
SHERMAN, N.
Children's Drawings (Complete)
SOMERS, H.
Three Sonnets
Sonata No. 4
TREMBLAY, G.
Pièces pour piano
Phases AND Réseaux
TURNER, R.
Sonata Lyrica
WEINSWEIG, J.
Sonata
WUENSCH, G.
Esquisse
Sonatina in D (1977) (Complete)
Sonatine (1992) (Complete)
Variations, Op. 90 (Complete)

ASSOCIATE
Voice (Performer)

Length of Examination: 75 minutes

Examination Fee: Please consult the current examination application form for the schedule of fees.

Co-requisites: Successful completion of THREE written examinations is required for the awarding of the Associate (Performer) Diploma, as follows:

Theory 7(A),   Theory 7(B),   History 7

Marking

Section	Requirement	Total Mark Possible	Minimum Mark Required
A	TEN ASSOCIATE LIST PIECES		
	To be performed from memory		
	ONE piece from List A	10	6.5
	ONE piece from List B	10	6.5
	ONE piece from List C	10	6.5
	ONE piece from List D	12	7.8
	ONE piece from List E	12	7.8
	TWO pieces from List F (2 x 10 marks)	20	13.0
	ONE piece from List G	10	6.5
	TWO pieces of the candidates own choice (2 x 8 marks)	16	10.4
	TOTAL MARK FOR THIS SECTION	100%	70%
B	TECHNICAL TESTS	Pass/Fail	Pass
	VOCALISES	Pass/Fail	Pass
	SIGHT READING	Pass/Fail	Pass
	Rhythm Pattern		
	Vocal Passage (unaccompanied)		
	Vocal Passage (accompanied)		
	AURAL TESTS	Pass/Fail	Pass
C	OVER-ALL TOTAL	100%	70%

Candidates must obtain:

a) A minimum mark in **each** of the List pieces as specified under Section A.

b) A "Pass" in each section of the Technical Tests & Musicianship Skills as listed under Section B. A candidate will be exempt from these tests in any sections(s) in which he/she received the minimum mark in the Grade 10 Conservatory Canada examination. (See Regulation IV. 7 given above.)

c) A minimum over-all average mark of 70%.

Candidates who fail to obtain the minimum grade in one or more of the requirements listed above (under a, b, or c) shall be required to repeat the ENTIRE EXAMINATION at a subsequent session.

REQUIREMENTS

A) Pieces

Candidates must be prepared to sing from memory a total of TEN pieces, chosen as follows:

List A (Baroque Period)	Choose ONE song/aria from a cantata or masque or opera from the Baroque Period, but NOT from an oratorio, passion, mass or canticle. May be sung in any language.
List B (German Lied)	Choose ONE Lied from either the Classical or the Romantic periods. Must be sung in German.
List C (Art Song)	Choose ONE French Art Song. Must be sung in French.
List D (Aria from Choral Work)	Choose ONE aria from an oratorio, passion, mass or canticle, but NOT from a Baroque cantata, masque, or opera. Must be sung in the original language.
List E (Aria from an Opera)	Choose ONE aria from any opera, any period (except Baroque). Must be sung in the original language.

NOTE: At least one aria from List D or List E must include a preceding recitative.

List F (Solo Songs)	Choose ANY TWO solo songs from the late-Romantic period or 20th Century (but not by a Canadian composer). May be sung in any language.
List G (Canadian work)	Choose ONE song by a Canadian composer. Must be sung in the original language.
Own Choice	Choose ANY TWO songs of the candidate's own choice, providing they do not appear in Lists for previous grades.

Pieces should be chosen to contrast in style, key, tempo, mood, etc. The complete program must be chosen so as to include TEN different composers, and at least one piece in each of the following languages: German, French, Italian, and English. All pieces must be performed from memory.

Pieces may be chosen from the Lists or candidates may choose their own repertoire from pieces not included in this Syllabus but of equal difficulty to those given in the Lists. Pieces that appear in Lists for previous Grades *(Voice Syllabus, 1999 edition)* may not be used. Candidates are reminded that own-choice pieces that are substituted for List pieces are classified as *Irregular List Pieces* and must be submitted to the Office of the Registrar for approval in accordance with Regulation IV.4 given above.

B) Technical & Musicianship Tests

Vocalises

Prepare ANY TWO (one major AND one minor key), each demonstrating a different technical skill, chosen from:

Concone, Op. 12:	Panofka, Op. 81	Bordogni, 36 Vocalises
Choose ANY ONE	Choose ANY ONE of Nos. 18-24	Choose ANY ONE of Nos. 2, 4, 6, 8, 9, 11, 14, 16, 18

Vocalises must be sung to the vowels **ah [a], ay [e], ee [i], oh [o], oo [u]**, changing them throughout the vocalise. Each vowel must be used. Memorization is encouraged but is NOT required.

Technical Exercises

Candidates must be prepared to sing any or all of the exercises given below, in the following manner:

i) sung to vowels

ah [a], ay [e], ee [i], oh [o], oo [u],

as requested by the examiner. Though the tonic sol-fa names may be used to learn these exercises, candidates may NOT sing using sol-fa names in the examination.

ii) sung without accompaniment. The examiner will give the lower TONIC note. Exercises may be transposed from the keys given below into keys suitable to the candidate's voice range. The examiner may give a different starting pitch for each exercise.

iv) metronome markings should be regarded as *minimum* speeds.

v) expression markings on the score must be observed.

vi) all exercises must be sung in a single breath unless a breath mark is indicated in the score by a comma.

vii) A slur has been used to indicate legato singing. Staccato markings have been used to indicate staccato singing.

VOICE (Performer)

Sight Reading

Candidates are required to perform at sight a) a rhythmic exercise and b) a passage of vocal score as described below. The candidate will be given a brief period to scan the score before beginning to sing. Candidates must perform the rhythm section without counting aloud. It is recommended that candidates maintain a steady beat, and avoid the unnecessary repetition caused by attempting to correct errors during the performance.

Before the candidate attempts to sing the unaccompanied vocal passage, the Examiner will play on the piano a I-IV-V-I chord progression (with the leading-note to tonic in the upper part) to establish the key and tonality. No starting note will be given.

a) Rhythm	b) Vocal Passage

To tap, clap or play on one note (at the candidate's choice) a rhythm in simple or compound time. May include syncopated rhythms, changing-meters, irregular meters, and complex patterns.
 	
 Length   4-8 bars
 Time signature   any simple or compound time
 Note values   variety of values including ties
 Rest values   variety of values
	To sing at sight TWO vocal passages, in English, about equal in difficulty to pieces at the Grade 6 level.
	    i) unaccompanied, using vowels. (8-12 bars)
	    ii) accompanied, using the text given on the score (16-24 bars)
	 Major AND Minor keys
	 Simple modulations
	 Beginning on ANY note of the scale

Example: a) Rhythm

Aural Tests

The candidate will be required:

i)   at the candidate's choice, to play back OR sing back to any vowel, the **lower** part of a two-part phrase in a major key, after the Examiner has:

       ✓ named the key [up to and including three sharps or flats]
       ✓ played the 4-note chord on the tonic in solid form
       ✓ played the passage twice.

The parts may begin on ANY note of the tonic chord. Following is the approximate level of difficulty:

ii)   to identify any of the following intervals after the Examiner has played each one once. Intervals may be played in melodic (broken) form OR harmonic (solid) form.

ABOVE a note	**BELOW a note**
major and minor 2nd	*major and minor 2nd*
major and minor 3rd	*major and minor 3rd*
perfect 4th	*perfect 4th*
augmented 4th (diminished 5th)	*augmented 4th (diminished 5th)*
perfect 5th	*perfect 5th*
major and minor 6th	*major and minor 6th*
major and minor 7th	*major and minor 7th*
perfect octave	*perfect octave*

iii)   to identify any of the following 4-note chords after each has been played once by the Examiner.
        major and *minor* chords: root position and first or second inversion [to be played in solid form, close position]
        dominant 7th chords: root position or any inversion [to be played in solid form, close position]
        diminished 7th chords: root position only [to be played in solid form, open (SATB) position]

iv)   to state whether a short piece in *chorale* style is in a *major* or a *minor* key, and whether the final cadence and all internal cadences are **Perfect** (V-I), **Imperfect** (I-V, II-V, IV-V), **Plagal** (IV-I), or **Interrupted/Deceptive** (V-VI). The Examiner will play the passage TWICE; the first time straight through without interruption, the second time stopping at cadence points for the candidate to identify them.

ASSOCIATE
Voice (Teacher)

Length of Examination: 75 minutes

Examination Fee: Please consult the current examination application form for the schedule of fees.

Co-requisites: Successful completion of FOUR written examinations is required for the awarding of the Associate (Teacher) Diploma, as follows:
Theory 7(A),   Theory 7(B),   History 7,   Pedagogy 7

Marking

Section	Requirement	Total Mark Possible	Minimum Mark Required
A	I. SIX ASSOCIATE LIST PIECES To be performed from memory 1. TWO pieces from any TWO of Lists A, B, C 2. ONE piece from List D 3. ONE operatic aria from List E 4. ONE 20th-century piece (not Canadian) from List F 5. ONE from List G (Canadian) TOTAL MARK FOR THIS SECTION	 12 6 6 6 6 36	 23.4
	II. ELEVEN PIECES Chosen from Grades 2-10 Repertoire Lists Grades 2, 4, 6 Grades 8-9 Grade 10 (List D) TOTAL MARK FOR THIS SECTION	 7 7 6 20	 13.0
B	TECHNICAL TESTS	10	6.5
	SIGHT READING Rhythm Pattern Vocal Passage (unaccompanied) Vocal Passage (accompanied)	6	3.9
	AURAL TESTS	8	5.2
C	VIVA VOCE	20	13
D	OVER-ALL TOTAL	100%	70%

Candidates must obtain:

a) The total minimum mark in each of the Associate List pieces and the Graded Repertoire pieces as specified under Section A.

b) The minimum mark in each of Technical Tests, Sight Reading, and Aural Tests as listed under Section B.

c) The minimum mark in Viva Voce as specified under Section C.

d) A minimum over-all average mark of 70%

Candidates who fail to achieve the required minimum mark in any section(s) (A, B or C) will be given conditional status in that section and must complete successfully a Supplemental Examination in the conditioned section(s) within twelve months of the original examination. Candidates who fail to achieve the required minimum over-all average mark of 70% will not be eligible for supplemental examinations and will be required to repeat the ENTIRE EXAMINATION at a subsequent session.

VOICE (Teacher)

REQUIREMENTS

A) Pieces

Candidates must be prepared to perform a total of SEVENTEEN pieces chosen as follows:

I. SIX Associate level pieces, to be performed from memory, chosen to include at least two languages other than English, as follows:

    1) Any TWO pieces chosen from any two of List A, List B, List C.

    2) ONE aria chosen from List D: a solo movement from a major choral work (e.g. oratorio, passion, mass, canticle) from any period.

    3) ONE operatic aria chosen from List E: any language or period.
        NOTE: At least ONE of the arias chosen from List D and List E must include a preceding recitative.

    4) ONE piece chosen from List F: 20th-century but NOT Canadian.

    5) ONE piece chosen from List G: Canadian composition.

II. ELEVEN pieces from Grade 2 through Grade 10 repertoire Lists of Conservatory Canada's Voice Syllabus (1999 edition). Memorization is not required.

Candidates must be familiar with Conservatory Canada's voice repertoire books, the *New Millennium Series*, and at least five of the eleven pieces must be chosen from this series. *(This regulation comes into effect beginning with the February 2000 session and following. It is NOT in effect for the February 1999 and June 1999 examination sessions.)*

Pieces must be chosen as follows:

    1) ONE piece from Grade 10, List D

    2) FOUR pieces, TWO from Grade 8 and TWO from Grade 9 repertoire, chosen as follows:

        ANY ONE from List A
        ANY ONE from List B
        ANY ONE from List C
        ANY ONE from List D

    3) SIX pieces, one from each of Grades 2-7 repertoire, chosen to include THREE pieces from List A and THREE pieces from List B:

Your eleven choices should comprise a well-balanced program of contrasting styles, keys, moods, tempo and text, and should include pieces by at least EIGHT different composers.

NOTE: Candidates must present to the Examiner a complete list of the eleven pieces prepared; however, the examiner may not necessarily hear every work on the list.

B) Technique & Musicianship Skills

Technical Tests

Candidates must be prepared to sing any or all of the exercises given below, in the following manner:

i) sung to vowels

ah [a], ay [e], ee [i], oh [o], oo [u],

as requested by the examiner. Though the tonic sol-fa names may be used to learn these exercises, candidates may NOT sing using sol-fa names in the examination.

ii) sung without accompaniment. The examiner will give the lower TONIC note. Exercises may be transposed from the keys given below into keys suitable to the candidate's voice range. The examiner may give a different starting pitch for each exercise.

iv) metronome markings should be regarded as *minimum* speeds.

v) expression markings on the score must be observed.

vi) all exercises must be sung in a single breath unless a breath mark is indicated in the score by a comma.

vii) A slur has been used to indicate legato singing. Staccato markings have been used to indicate staccato singing.

Sight Reading

Candidates are required to perform at sight
  - a) a rhythmic exercise
  - b) a passage of vocal score (without accompaniment)
  - c) a passage of vocal score (with piano accompaniment)

The candidate will be given a brief period to scan the score before beginning to sing. However, candidates are not permitted to hum the melody while scanning. Candidates must perform the rhythm section without counting aloud. It is recommended that candidates maintain a steady beat, and avoid the unnecessary repetition caused by attempting to correct errors during the performance.

Before the candidate attempts to sing the vocal passage, the Examiner will play on the piano a I-IV-V-I chord progression (with the leading-note to tonic in the upper part) to establish the key and tonality. No starting note will be given.

Rhythm	*Vocal Passage*

To tap, clap or play on one note (at the candidate's choice) a rhythm in simple, compound or irregular time. May include syncopated rhythms, changing-meters, irregular meters, and complex patterns.
 	
 Length   4-8 bars
 Note values   variety of values including ties
 Rest values   variety of values
	To sing at sight TWO vocal passages, in English, each about equal in difficulty to songs at the Grade 8 level.
	    i) without accompaniment, using vowels (12-16 bars)
	    ii) with piano accompaniment, using the text given on the score (16-24 bars)
	 Major AND Minor keys
	 Simple modulations
	 Beginning on ANY note of the scale

Example: a) Rhythm

Aural Tests

i) To play back **on the piano** both parts of a two-part phrase (approximately four bars) in either a major or a minor key, after the examiner has named the key, given the tonic chord, and played the passage twice.

Example:

ii) Identify melodic intervals after each has been played once (either ascending or descending). All major, minor, and perfect intervals, and also augmented 4th and major or minor 9th.

iii) Identify time signatures of short passages of music after each has been played once.

iv) Identify, by symbols, chord progressions in root position only employed in a four-bar phrase, in major key only, beginning on the tonic. Chords on the I, ii, IV, V, vi, and vii⁰₆, and a cadential 6/4 may be used. The examiner will play the tonic chord and then will play the entire phrase twice. During the second playing the examiner will stop after each chord for the candidate to identify the harmony.

C) Viva Voce

1) Candidates are required to demonstrate a knowledge of methods of teaching including:

     a) the first lesson;

     b) practising methods, technical routine, aural training, sight reading, memorization;

     c) the principles of proper voice production, including breath control, resonance, focus of tone and diction;

     d) the classification of voices;

     e) the teaching of recitative, technique and vocalises;

     f) stylistic interpretation and other musical matters in general.

VOICE (Teacher)

2) Candidates should have a strong practical acquaintance with a variety of beginner's books, teaching material, repertoire for more advanced levels, technical exercises both for examination requirements (i.e. scales, chords, arpeggios, etc.) and for non-examination purposes (i.e. for solving specific technical difficulties presented by the repertoire, etc.).

3) Candidates must be prepared to perform any of those List pieces (Grades 2 - 10) as presented by the candidate for performance in the practical portion of this examination. Candidates must play their own piano accompaniment for those pieces from Grades 2-7, but may choose, if they wish, to have a piano accompanist play for those pieces from Grades 8-10). Candidates must also be prepared to demonstrate the teaching of any of those pieces (Grades 2-10):

   a) to show how the piece should be introduced to the student;

   b) to recognize any special difficulties in the piece and to demonstrate how each might be overcome;

   c) to demonstrate the teaching of the notation, time, rhythm, tone, dynamics, interpretation, style and form of the piece;

   d) a demonstration lesson of one piece chosen by the examiner. The examiner may perform the piece, introducing certain errors, and the candidate will be expected to detect such errors and to demonstrate how to correct them.

4) The candidate should have a secure and broad knowledge of musical style and interpretation as applied to vocal literature, including dynamics, phrasing, articulation, tempo, rhythm, ornamentation, etc.

5) The candidate must display a basic knowledge of Canadian composers and compositions.

Associate Voice List Pieces

LIST A
Baroque

BACH, J.S.
  Cantatas (soprano)
    Choose ANY ONE of
      No. 49   Ich bin herrlich, ich bin schön
      No. 51   Jauchzet Gott in allen Landen
      No. 84   Ich bin vergnügt
      No. 187   Gott versorget alles Leben
      No. 202   Sich üben im Lieben
      No. 202   Weichet nur betrübte Schatten
      No. 208   Schafe können sicher weiden
      No. 210   Ruhet hie, matte Töne
  Cantatas (mezzo soprano/alto)
    Choose ANY ONE of
      No. 29   Hallelujah Stärk und Macht
      No. 35   Gott hat alles wohlgemacht
      No. 114   Du machst, O Tod
      No. 129   Gelobet sei der Herr
      No. 151   Süsser Trost, mein Jesu
  Cantatas (tenor)
    Choose ANY ONE of
      No. 61   Komm Jesu
      No. 70   Hebt euer Haupt empor
      No. 75   Mein Jesu soll mein Alles sein
  Cantatas (bass/baritone)
    Choose ANY ONE of
      No. 27   Gute Nacht
      No. 49   Ich geh und suche
      No. 21   Hat man nicht mit seinen Kindern
CIMAROSA, D.
  Nel lasciarti, O prence amato
GREENE, M.
  Orpheus with his Lute
HÄNDEL, G.F.
  Acis and Galatea
    Choose ANY Recitative AND aria
    Recit: Ye verdant plains AND
    Aria: Hush, ye pretty warbling
    Recit: Lo! Here my love AND
    Aria: Love in her eyes sits
    Recit: O didst thou know AND

  Aria: As when the dove
  Recit: I rage, I melt AND
  Aria: O ruddier than the cherry
  Recit: His hideous love AND
  Aria: Love sounds th'alarm
  Atalanta
    Choose ANY ONE of
      Come alla tortorella
      Laschia ch'io parta solo
  Guilio Cesare
    Recit: Dall'ondoso periglio AND
    Aria: Aure, deh, per pieta
    Recit: E pur così in un giorno AND
    Aria: Piangero la sorte mia
  Ottone
    Vinte e l'amor
  Psalm 112
    Excelsus super omnes
  Rodelinda
    Confusa si miri
  Tamerlano
    Ben che mi sprezzi
PURCELL, H.
  Arise, ye subterranean winds
  Here let my life
  The Blessed Virgin's Expostulation
  See the Heavens smile (*The Fairy Queen*)
  Sweeter than roses
  Ye twice ten hundred deities
  Three Divine Hymns (arr. Britten)
    Choose ANY ONE of
      Lord what is man?
      We sing to Him
SCARLATTI, A.
  Five Songs (arr. Moriarty)
    Choose ANY TWO
  Ten Arias (Schirmer)
      Non vi vorrei conoscere
      Nell' aspro mio dolor

LIST B
Lieder

BRAHMS, J.
  Album I (Peters)
    Choose ANY ONE of
      An ein Veilchen
      Feldeinsamkeit
  Album II (Peters)
    Choose ANY ONE of
      Ruhe, Süssliebchen
      Sind es Schmerzen
      Von ewiger Liebe
      Wie soll ich die Freude
  Album III (Peters)
    Die Trauernde

  Album IV (Peters)
    Verrat
  Zigeunerlieder (Dover)
    Choose ANY TWO
LISZT, F.
  Thirty Songs (Dover)
    Choose ANY ONE of
      Der König von Thule
      Die Lorelei
      Die Vätergruft
      Kling leise, mein Lied
      Mignon's Lied

VOICE (Repertoire)

MAHLER, G.
24 Songs, I (International)
Wer hat dies Liedlein
24 Songs, II (International)
Wo die schönen Trompeten
24 Songs, IV (International)
Choose ANY ONE of
Ich bin der Welt abhanden
Um Mitternacht
Rheinlegendchen
MOZART, W.A.
Abendempfindung
SCHUBERT, F.
Album I (Peters)
Choose ANY ONE of
Am Meer
Aufenthalt
Der Doppelgänger
Die junge Nonne
Gretchen am Spinnrade
Album II (Peters)
Choose ANY ONE of
Des Fischer's Liebesglück
Die Allmacht
Gruppe aus dem Tartarus
Suleika (1 or 2)
Album IV (Peters)
Heimliches Lieben
Album VI (Peters)
An die Apfelbäume
SCHUMANN, R.
Album I (Peters)
Ich Grolle Nicht
Album II (Peters)
Choose ANY ONE of
Aufträge
Belsatzar
Der Spielmann
Schöne Wiege meiner Leiden

Album III (Peters)
Abendlied
STRAUSS, R.
27 Songs (International)
Choose ANY ONE of
Ach Lieb, ich muss
Befreit
Cäcilie
Heimliche Aufforderung
Nachtgang
Nichts
Schlagende Herzen
Seitdem dein Aug'
Ständchen
Zueignung
WAGNER, R.
Wesendonk Lieder (Dover)
Choose ANY ONE of
Der Engel
Im Treibhaus
Stehe Still!
Träume
WOLF, H.
65 Songs (International)
Choose ANY ONE of
Anakreon's Grab
Er ist's
Ich hab in Penna
Nachtzauber
Verschwiegene Liebe
Zur Ruh
Album II (Peters)
Choose ANY ONE of
Ihr jungen Leute
Die Bekehrte
Die Spröde
Michelangelo Lieder (Peters)
Fühlt meine Seele

LIST C
French Art Songs

BERLIOZ, H.
Les Nuits d'Eté
Choose ANY ONE
CHAUSSON, E.
20 Songs (International)
Choose ANY ONE of
Le Caravane
Nanny
Le temps de Lilas
Sérénade
L'Aveu
Cantiques à l'Epouse
DEBUSSY, C.
Ariettes oubliées
Choose ANY ONE
(except C'est l'extase and Il pleure dans mon coeur)
Fêtes Galantes
Choose ANY ONE
Le jet d'eau
Recueillment

Noel des Enfants (International)
DUPARC, H.
11 Songs (International)
Choose ANY ONE of
Chanson triste
L'invitation au voyage
La vie antérieure
Le manoir de Rosemonde
Phidylé
Soupir
FAURÉ, G.
30 Songs (International)
Choose ANY ONE of
Automne
Fleur jetée
L'hiver a cessé
Soir
Sylvie
FRANCK, C.
La procession (Schirmer)

VOICE (Repertoire)

LIST D
Oratorio, Passion, etc.

For Soprano	For Mezzo-Soprano or Contralto

BACH, J.S.
Christmas Oratorio
Choose ANY ONE of
Flösst, mein Heiland
Nur ein Wink
St. John Passion
Ich folge Dir gleichfalls
St. Matthew Passion
Choose ANY ONE of
Blute nur, du liebes Herz
Recit: Wiewohl mein Herz AND
Aria: Ich will Dir mein Herze
Recit: Er hat uns allen wohlgetan AND
Aria: Aus Liebe will mein Heiland
Mass in B minor
Laudamus te
ELGAR, E.
The Apostles
The voice of Thy watchman
HÄNDEL, G.F.
Esther
Hallelujah
Israel in Egypt
Thou didst blow with the wind
Jephtha
Recit: Ye sacred priests AND
Aria: Farewell, ye limpid springs
Joshua
O had I Jubal's lyre
Judas Maccabaeus
Choose ANY ONE of
So shall the lute and harp
Come, ever smiling liberty
Wise men, flau'ring
Recit: O let eternal honours AND
Aria: From mighty kings
Messiah
Choose ANY ONE of
I know that my Redeemer
If God be for us
Rejoice greatly
Samson
Let the bright Seraphim
Solomon
Bless'd the day
HAYDN, F.J.
The Creation
Choose ANY ONE of
Recit: And God said AND
Aria: With verdure clad
The Seasons
O how pleasing
MENDELSSOHN, F.
Elijah
Hear ye, Israel

BACH, J.S.
Christmas Oratorio
Choose ANY ONE of
Bereite dich, Zion
Schlafe, mein Liebster
Magnificat
Choose ANY ONE of
Esurientes emplevit bonis
Et exultavit
Mass in B minor
Choose ANY ONE of
Agnus Dei
Qui Sedes
St. John Passion
Choose ANY ONE of
Es ist vollbracht
Von den Stricken
St. Matthew Passion
Choose ANY ONE of
Recit: Du lieber Heiland AND
Aria: Buss und Reu
Recit: Erbarm es Gott AND
Aria: Können Tränen
ELGAR, E.
The Dream of Gerontius
Choose ANY ONE of
Softly and gently, dearly ransomed soul
The Angel's Song (*My work is done*)
HÄNDEL, G.F.
Israel in Egypt
Thou shalt bring them in
Jeptha
In gentle murmurs
Judas Maccabaeus
Father of Heaven
Messiah
Choose ANY ONE of
He was despised
Recit: Behold! a Virgin AND
Aria: O thou that tellest
Samson
Choose ANY ONE of
Return, O God of Hosts
The holy one of Israel
Saul
Lord, whose mercies
Semele
Hence, Iris, hence away
Theodora
Lord, to Thee each night
MENDELSSOHN, F.
Elijah
O rest in the Lord
ROSSINI, G.
Stabat Mater
Fac ut Portem

VOICE (Repertoire)

For Tenor

BACH, J.S.
Christmas Oratorio
  Choose ANY ONE of
    Frohe Hirten, eilt
    Ich will nur dir
    Recit: So geht! Genug AND
    Aria: Nun mögt ihr Stolzen
Magnificat
  Deposuit potentes
Mass in B minor
  Benedictus
St. John Passion
  Choose ANY ONE of
    Ach, mein Sinn
    Erwäge, wie sein
St. Matthew Passion
  Geduld

BEETHOVEN, L. Van
Christ on the Mount of Olives
  Jehova, du mein Vater! Meine Seele ist erschüttert

ELGAR, E.
The Dream of Gerontius
  Choose ANY ONE of
    Jesu, Maria I am near to death
    Sanctus fortis

HÄNDEL, G.F.
Hercules
  From celestial seats
Israel in Egypt
  The enemy said
Jephtha
  Recit: Deeper and deeper AND
  Aria: Waft her, angels
Judas Maccabaeus
  Choose ANY ONE of
    Recit: 'Tis well my friends AND
    Aria: Call forth Thy powers
    Recit: Thanks to my brethren AND
    Aria: How vain is man
    Sound an alarm
    With honour let desert
Messiah
  Choose ANY ONE of
    Recit: The voice of Him that crieth AND
    Aria: Every valley shall be exalted
    Recit: Thy rebuke has broken AND
    Aria: Behold and see
    Recit: He was cut off AND
    Aria: But thou didst not leave
    Recit: He that dwelleth AND
    Aria: Thou shalt break them
Occasional Oratorio
  Choose ANY ONE of
    Jehovah! to my words
    Then will I Jehovah's praise
Samson
  Choose ANY ONE of
    Thus when the sun
    Recit: My grief for this AND
    Aria: Why does the God
Saul
  Sin not, O King
Susanna
  Recit: Tyrannic love AND
  Aria: Ye verdant hills

HAYDN, F.J.
The Creation
  Recit: And God created man AND
  Aria: In native worth
The Seasons
  The Traveller stands

MENDELSSOHN, F.
Elijah
  Choose ANY ONE of
    Recit: Ye people rend your hearts AND
    Aria: If with all your hearts
    Then shall the righteous shine
St. Paul
  Be thou faithful unto death

ROSSINI, G.
Stabat Mater
  Cujus animam
Messe Solemnelle
  Domine Deus

VERDI, G.
Requiem
  Qui Miriam absolvisti

For Baritone or Bass

BACH, J.S.
Christmas Oratorio
  Choose ANY ONE of
    Grosser Herr und starker
    Erleucht auch meine finstre
Mass in B minor
  Et in spiritum sanctum
St. Matthew Passion
  Choose ANY ONE of
    Gerne will ich mich
    Gebt mir meinen Jesum
    Recit: Ja freilich will AND
    Aria: Komm, süsses Kreuz
Magnificat
  Quia fecit mihi magna

ELGAR, E.
The Dream of Gerontius
  Jesu! By that shuddering dread

HÄNDEL, G.F.
Alexander's Feast
  Revenge, Timotheus cries
Deborah
  Tears such as tender
Dettinger Te Deum
  Choose ANY ONE of
    Vouchsafe, O Lord
    When Thou tookest upon Thee
Esther
  Turn not, O Queen
Joshua
  Choose ANY ONE of
    See the raging flames
    Shall I in Mamre's
Judas Maccabaeus
  Choose ANY ONE of
    Recit: I feel the Deity AND
    Aria: Arm ye brave
    Recit: Be comforted AND
    Aria: The Lord worketh
    Recit: Enough! To Heaven AND

Aria: With pious hearts
Messiah
  Choose ANY ONE of
    Recit: For behold, darkness AND
    Aria: The people that walked in darkness
    Recit: Behold, I tell you a mystery AND
    Aria: The trumpet shall sound
    Why do the nations
Samson
  Choose ANY ONE of
    Honour and arms
    How willing my paternal love
    Thy glorious deeds
Semele
  Leave me, loathsome light

HAYDN, F.J.

The Creation
  Recit: And God said AND
  Aria: Rolling in foaming
The Seasons
  With joy th'impatient
MENDELSSOHN, F.
Elijah
  It is enough
St. Paul
  Choose ANY ONE of
    Consume them all
    O God, have mercy
ROSSINI, G.
Stabat Mater
  Pro peccatis
Messe Solemnelle
  Quoniam tu solus

LIST E
Opera

For Soprano

BEETHOVEN, L. von
Fidelio
  O, wär ich schön
BELLINI, V.
Norma
  Casta Diva [sing cavatina only]
BIZET, G.
Carmen
  Je dis que rien
Les Pêcheurs de Perles
  Choose ANY ONE of
    Comee autrefois
    Me voila seule dans la nuit
BOITO, A
Mefistofele
  L'altra notte in fondo
BRITTEN, B.
Peter Grimes
  Embroidery in Childhood
CATALANI, A.
La Wally
  Ebben? N'andro lontana
CHARPENTIER, G.
Louise
  Depuis le jour
DEBUSSY, C.
L'Enfant Prodigue
  Air de Lia
DONIZETTI, G.
Lucia di Lammermoor
  Regnava nel silenzio
Don Pasquali
  So anch'io la virtu
La Fille du Regiment
  Chacun le Sait
DVORAK, A.
Russalka
  Song to the Moon

GLUCK, C. W. von
Alceste
  Divinités du Styx
GOUNOD, C.
Faust
  Jewel Song
MASCAGNI, P.
Cavalleria Rusticana
  Voi lo sapete, O mamma
MASSENET, J.
Le Cid
  Pleurez, mes yeux
Manon
  Gavotte
MENOTTI, G-C
Amelia al Ballo
  Romanza [Amelia's Aria]
The Consul
  To this we've come
MEYERBEER, G.
Dinorah
  Ombra leggiera
MOORE, D.
The Ballad of Baby Doe
  Choose ANY ONE of
    Dearest Mama
    Willow Song
MOZART, W.A.
Cosi fan Tutte
  Choose ANY ONE of
    Come scoglio
    E amore un ladroncello
    Per pietà ben mio perdona
Die Entführung aus dem Serail
  Choose ANY ONE of
    Ach ich liebte
    Martern aller Arten
    Welche Wonne
Don Giovanni
  Choose ANY ONE of
    Recit: Un quali eccessi AND
    Aria: Mi tradi quel alma

VOICE (Repertoire)

Recit: Crudele? Ah no AND
Aria: Non mi dir
Idomeneo
  Choose ANY ONE of
    Idol mio, se ritoso altro
    Recit: O smania, O furie! AND
    Aria: D'oreste, d'ajace!
La Clemenza di Tito
  Choose ANY ONE of
    Deh per questo istante solo
    Saltro che lagrime
Le Nozze di Figaro
  Choose ANY ONE of
    Recit: Guinse alfin il momento AND
    Aria: Deh vieni non tardar
    Recit: E Susanna non vien AND
    Aria: Dove sono
    Porgi amor
The Impressario
  Choose ANY ONE of
    Bester Jüngling
    Da schlägt die
Die Zauberflote
  Choose ANY ONE of
    Ach, ich fühls
    Der Hölle Rache

PONCHIELLI, A.
La Gioconda
  Suicido!

PUCCINI, G.
La Bohème
  Choose ANY ONE of
    Donde lieta usci
    Si, mi chiamano Mimi
    Quando me'n vo
Gianni Schicchi
  O mio babbino caro
Madama Butterfly
  Choose ANY ONE of
    Ancora un passo
    Un bel di vedremo
Manon Lescaut
  In quelle trine morbide
Tosca
  Vissi d'arte

OFFENBACH, J.
Les Contes d'Hoffman
  Choose ANY ONE of
    Les oiseaux dans la charmille
    Elle a fui, la tourterelle

ROSSINI, G
Semiramide
  Recit: Bel raggio lusinghier AND
  Aria: Dolce pensiero

STRAVINSKY, I.
The Rake's Progress
  Choose ANY ONE of
    Quietly, Night
    I go to him

VERDI, G.
Aida
  Recit: Qui Radamès verrà AND
  Aria: O patria mia
Il Trovatore
  Recit: Timor di me AND
  Aria: D'amor sull' alli rose
La Forza del Destino
  Pace, pace mio Dio

La Traviata
  Choose ANY ONE of
    Addio del passato
    Recit: È strano AND
    Aria: Ah, forse lui
Otello
  Choose ANY ONE of
    Ave Maria
    Recit: Mi parea AND
    Aria: Piangea cantando
Rigoletto
  Caro nome

WAGNER, R.
Lohengrin
  Elsa's Traum
Tannhäuser
  Choose ANY ONE of
    Dich, teure Halle
    Allmächt'ge Jungfrau

Weber, C.M. von
Der Freischütz
  Recit: Wie nahte mir der Schlummer AND
  Aria: Leise, leise fromme Weise

For Mezzo-soprano or Contralto

BIZET, G.
Carmen
  Choose ANY ONE of
    Habanera
    Seguidilla

BRITTEN, B.
The Rape of Lucretia
  The Flower Song

DE FALLA, M.
La Vida Breve
  Vivan los que rien

DONIZETTI, G.
La Favorita
  O mio Fernando

GLUCK, C.W. von
Orfeo
  Che farò senza Euridice

GOUNOD, C.
Faust
  Faites-lui mes aveux
Roméo et Juliette
  Recit: Depuis hier je cherche AND
  Aria: Que fais-tu blanche

MEYERBEER, G.
Le Prophète
  Ah! mon fils
Les Huguenots
  Nobles seigneurs, salut!

MOZART, W.A.
Cosi Fan Tutti
  Recit: Ah! Scostati, paventa il tristo effetto AND
  Aria: Smanie implacabili

MOUSSORGSKY, M.
Boris Godunov
  Life is empty

PONCHIELLI, A.
La Gioconda
  Voce de donna

VOICE (Repertoire)

ROSSINI, G
Il Barbiere de Siviglia
Una voce poco fa
La Cenerentola
Recit: Nacqui All'affanno AND
Aria: Non piu mesta
Semiramide
In si Barbara
SAINT-SAËNS, C.
Samson et Dalila
Choose ANY ONE of
Amour, viens aider
Mon coeur s'ouvre
Printemps qui commence
THOMAS, A.
Mignon
Connais-tu le pays
TCHAIKOWSKY, P.I.
Jeanne d'Arc
Adieu, fôrets
VERDI, G.
Don Carlo
O don fatale
Il Travatore
Stride la vampa
Un Ballo in Maschera
Re dell'abisso
WAGNER, R.
Parsifal
Ich sah das Kind
Das Rheingold
Erda's Warnung

For Tenor

BIZET, G.
Carmen
La fleur que tu m'avais jetee
La Jolie Fille de Perth
A la voix d'un amant
Les Pêcheurs de Perles
Je crois entendre encore
BRITTEN, B.
Peter Grimes
Peter's Dream
The Rape of Lucretia
The Ride
DONIZETTI, G.
Don Pasquale
Com' è gentil
L'Elisir d'Amore
Una furtiva lagrima
GIORDANO, V.
Fedora
Amor ti vieto
GOUNOD, C.
Faust
Recit: Quel trouble inconnu AND
Aria: Salut! Demeure chaste
Roméo et Juliette
Ah! léve-toi, soleil
LALO, E.
Le Roi d' Ys
Vainement, ma bien-aimée

LEONCAVALLO, R.
Pagliacci
Vesti la giubba
MASCAGNI, P.
Cavalleria Rusticana
O Lola, bianca come fior
MASSENET, J.
Manon
Choose ANY ONE of
Le Rêve
Ah! Fuyez douce image
Pourquoi me réveiller
MEYERBEER, G.
L'Africaine
Recit: Pays merveilleux AND
Aria: O paradis
MOZART, W.A.
Cosi fan Tutte
Un' aura amoroso
Die Entführung aus dem Serail
Choose ANY ONE of
Constanze! Dich wieder zu
Frisch zum Kampfe
Hier soll ich dich denn sehen
Ich baue ganz auf deine Stärke
Wenn der Freude Tränen
Don Giovanni
Choose ANY ONE of
Dalla sua pace
Il mio tesoro
Idomeneo
Fuor del mar
La Clemenza di Tito
Del più sublime soglio
Se all'impero
Die Zauberflöte
Dies Bildnis ist
PONCHIELLI, A.
La Gioconda
Cielo e mar!
PUCCINI, G.
La Bohème
Che gelida manina
La Fanciulla del West
Ch'ella mi creda
Manon Lescaut
Donna non vidi mai
Tosca
Choose ANY ONE of
E lucevan le stelle
Recondita armonia
Turandot
Nessun dorma
ROSSINI, G.
Il Barbière di Siviglia
Ecco ridente
L'Italiana in Algeri
Languir per una bella
VERDI, G.
Aida
Celeste Aida
Il Trovatore
Choose ANY ONE of
Ah sì, ben mio coll'essere
Di quella pira
La Forza del Destino
O tu che in seno agli angeli
La Traviata
De'miei bollenti spiriti

VOICE (Repertoire)

Rigoletto
Choose ANY ONE of
La donna è mobile
Questa o qualla

WAGNER, R.
Die Walküre
Winterstürme
Lohengrin
In fernem Land
Die Meistersinger
Walter's Preislied

WEBER, C.M., von
Der Freischütz
Durch die Wälder, durch die Auen

For Baritone or Bass

BIZET, G.
Carmen
Votre toast (Toreador's Song)
La Jolie Fille de Perth
Quand la flamme
Les Pêcheurs de Perles
O Nadir

DONIZETTI, G.
Don Pasquale
Bella siccome un angelo
La Favorite
Pour tant d'amour
Lucia di Lammermoor
Cruda, funesta smania

GIORDANO, U.
Andrea Chenier
Nemico della patria?

GOUNOD, C.
Faust
Choose ANY ONE of
Avant de quitter ces lieux
Le veau d'or

LEONCAVALLO, R.
Pagliacci
Prologue

MASSENET, J.
Hérodiade
Vision fugitive
Manon
Epouse quelque brave fille

MEYERBEER, G.
L'Africaine
Fille des rois

MOZART, W.A.
Cosi fan Tutte
Choose AnY ONE of
Donne mie, la fatte a tanti
Non siate ritrosi
Die Zauberflöte
Choose ANY ONE of
Der Vogelfänger bin ich ja
Ein Mädchen oder Weibchen
In diesen heil'gen Hallen
Don Giovanni
Choose ANY ONE of
Deh vieni alla finestra

Finchè han dal vino
Madamina! Il catalogo
Le Nozze di Figaro
Choose ANY ONE of
Non più andrai
Vedrò mentr'io sospiro

MOUSSORGSKY, M.
Boris Godunov
Choose ANY ONE of
Varlaam's Song
I have attained the highest power

PUCCINI, G.
La Bohème
Vecchia zimarra

ROSSINI, G.
Il Barbiere di Siviglia
Choose ANY ONE of
A un dottor della mia sorte
La calunnia
Largo al factotum
La Gazza Ladra
Il mio piano
L'Italiana in Algeri
Gia d'insolito Ardore

TCHAIKOVSKY, P.I.
Eugene Onegin
Gremin's Aria

VERDI, G.
Don Carlo
Choose ANY ONE of
Recit: Convien qui dirci addio AND
Aria: Per me giunto
Dormirò sol nel manto mio regal
Il Trovatore
Il balen del suo sorriso
I Vespri Siciliani
Recit: O patria, o cara patria AND
Aria: O, tu Palermo
La Traviata
Recit: Mio figlio! AND
Aria: Di Provenza il mar
Otello
Recit: Vanne, la tua meta AND
Aria: Credo in un Dio
Rigoletto
Recit: Si, la mia figlia AND
Aria: Cortigiani, vil razza
Simon Boccanegra
Recit: A te l'estremo addio AND
Aria: Il lacerato spirto
Un Ballo in Maschera
Recit: Alzati! Là tuo figlio AND
Aria: Eri tu

WAGNER, R.
Der fliegende Holländer
Die Frist ist um
Die Meistersinger
Choose ANY ONE of
Nun hört und versteht
Wahn! Wahn! (Sachs monologue)
Was duftet doch der Flieder
Tannhäuser
Recit: Wie Todesahnung AND
Aria: O du mein holder

LIST F
20th Century: Not Canadian

ADLER, S.
Chill of the Eve
Stormy Weather
The Wind
The Piper
ARGENTO, D.
Six Elizabethan Songs
Choose ANY ONE
BAKER, R.
The Heavenly Song (*Triptych*)
BARBER, S.
Three Songs, Op. 45
Choose ANY ONE
Selected Songs (Schirmer)
Choose ANY ONE of
I hear an army
Nuvoletto
Sleep now
The Queen's Face
Seven Songs (Chester)
Choose ANY ONE of
The White Peace
A Christmas Carol
The Enchanted Fiddle
Roundel
BEESON, J.
Death by Owl-/Eyes
To a Sinister Potato
BERG, A.
Sieben frühe Lieder (Universal)
Choose ANY ONE
Vier Lieder (Universal)
Choose ANY ONE
BERKELEY, L.
Five Poems (Auden)
Choose ANY ONE
Five Songs (de la Mare)
Choose ANY ONE
Five Chinese Songs
Choose ANY ONE of
Late Spring
People Hide their Love
The Riverside Village
BRITTEN, B.
Fish in the unruffled lakes
A Birthday Hansel
Choose ANY ONE
Les Illuminations
Choose ANY ONE of
Antique
Being Beauteous
Marina
Parade
Royante
Villes
Sechs Hölderlin Fragmente
Choose ANY ONE
Seven Sonnets of Michelangelo
Choose ANY ONE
Songs & Proverbs of Wm Blake
Choose ANY ONE

Songs from the Chinese
Choose ANY ONE
The Holy Sonnets of John Donne
Choose ANY ONE
The Poet's Echo
Choose ANY ONE
Tit for Tat
Choose ANY ONE
Who Are These Children?
Choose ANY ONE
CHABRIER, E.
Les Cigales
COPLAND, A.
Twelve Poems of Emily Dickinson
Choose ANY ONE of
Going to Heaven
Heart we will forget him
I've heard an organ talk
Why do they shut me out
I felt a funeral
The Chariot
DALLAPICCOLA, L.
La Primavera ha Venido
DE FALLA M.
Siete Canciones Populares Espanolas
Choose ANY ONE
DELIBES, L.
Les filles de Cadiz
DELIUS, F.
Il pleure dans mon coeur
Love's Philosophy
Morning Star
So white, so soft is she
To the Queen of my Heart
A Book of Songs
Choose ANY ONE of
Black Roses (Set 1)
The Nightingale (Set 2)
DELLO JOIO, N.
Un sonetto del Petrarca
ELGAR, E.
Sabbath morning at sea
Sea slumber song
FINZI, G.
Budmouth Dears
To Lizbie Browne (*Earth and Air and Rain*)
Dies Natalis
Choose ANY ONE of
Nos. 2, 3, 4, 5
FORD, E.
From the Four Seasons
Choose ANY ONE
GRANADOS, E.
Canciones Amatorias
Choose ANY ONE
GRIFFES, C.T.
Four Impressions
Choose ANY ONE
GURIDI, J.
Seis Canciones Castellanas
Choose ANY ONE

VOICE (Repertoire)

HINDEMITH, P.
Das Marienleben
  Choose ANY ONE of
    Argwohn Joseph's
    Geburt Maria
Deux Ballades
  Choose ANY ONE
Nine English Songs
  Choose ANY ONE of
    Echo
    The Wild Flower's Song
    Sing on there in the swamp

HODDINOTT, A.
Ancestor Worship
  Choose ANY ONE
Landscapes
  Choose ANY ONE

HOLST, G.
Vedic Hymns
  Choose ANY ONE
Three Songs of Contemplation
  Choose ANY ONE of
    Deidre
    Solitaire
    The Lost Cause

HONNEGER, A.
Les Cloches
Quatre Poemes
  Choose ANY ONE

IVES, C.
General Booth Enters into Heaven
An Election
Majority
On the Antipodes

McINTYRE, D.
Five Sonnets of Archibald Lampman
  Choose ANY ONE

MENOTTI, G.-C.
Canti Della Lontananza
  Choose ANY TWO

MOUSSORGSKY, M.
Songs and Dances of Death
  Choose ANY ONE

PIERNÉ, H>
Six Ballades Françaises
  Choose ANY ONE of
    Complainte des Arches
    La vie
    Les dernieres pensees

PINKHAM, D.
Elegy

POULENC, F.
Miroirs Brulants
  Choosee ANY ONE of
    Tu vois le feu du soir
    Je monnerai ton front
Quatre Poemes de Guillaume Appolinaire
  Choosee ANY ONE of
    Avant le Cinema
    Carte Postale
    L'Anguilla
    1904

RACHMANINOFF, S.
Harvest of Sorrows
Spring Waters
To the Children
Vocalise

RAVEL, M.
Scheherezade (Durand)
  Choose ANY ONE of
    Asie
    La flûte enchantée
Don Quichotte and Dulcinee
  Choose ANY ONE
Histoires naturelles
  Choose ANY ONE
Kaddisch (*Deux melodies Hebraiques*)

RESPIGHI, O.
Ballata
In Alto Mare
L'udir Talvolta
Nebbie
Pioggia

RODRIGO, J.
Cuatro Madrigales Amatorios
  Choose ANY ONE
Canciones
  Choosce ANY ONE of
    Soneto
    Romancillo
    i Un Home, San Antonio!

ROREM, N.
Cycle of Holy Songs
  Choose ANY TWO

RUBBRA, E.
Three Psalms
  Choose ANY ONE

SESSIONS, R.
New Vistas in Song
  On the beach at Fontana

SIBELIUS, J.
Black Roses
From the North
The Tryst

STANFORD, C.V.
Johneen
The Crow
The Pibroch

STRAVINSKY, I.
Pastorale
Trois Histoires pour Enfants
  Nos. 2 AND 3

THOMPSON, R.
Praises and Prayers

TIPPETT, M.
The Heart's Assurance Song
  Choose ANY ONE of
    The heart's assurance
    Compassion
    The Dancer
    Remember your lovers

TURINA
Homenaje A Lope de Vega
  Choose ANY ONE of
    Al vol de Fuente
    Quando tan hermosa as mira
    Si con mis deseos
Tres Poemas, Op. 81
  Choose ANY ONE

VAUGHAN WILLIAMS, R.
On Wenlock Edge
  Choose ANY ONE
Pilgrim's Progress
  Choose ANY ONE of

VOICE (Teacher)

The Bird's Song
Watchful's Song
The New Ghost
The Water Mill

WALTON, W.
A Song for the Lord Mayor's Table
Choose ANY ONE

LIST G
Canadian Compositions

ARCHER, V.
Three Biblical Songs
Choose ANY ONE
Two Songs for Soprano (1978)
SING BOTH Songs
BISSELL, K.
Four Songs (High Voice & Harp)
Choose ANY ONE of
  A Cradle Song
  To a Child Dancing in the Wind
  O do not love too long
  When you are old
Quatre Chansons
Choose ANY ONE
COLES, G.
Midnight (1971)
COULTHARD, J.
Nocturne
The Wise Lover
Spring Rhapsody
Choose ANY ONE
CRAWLEY, C.
Songs of Duke Redbird
Choose ANY THREE
FLEMING, R.
The Confession Stone
Choose ANY ONE
FORSYTH, M
Incantation
Three Metis Songs
Choose ANY ONE

FREEDMAN, W.
Anerca
Choose ANY ONE
HÉTU, J.
Les Clartes de la Nuit (1972)
Choose ANY ONE
MERCURE, P.
Dissidence (1955)
Choose ANY ONE
MORAWETZ, O.
I Love the Jocund Dance
Mother I cannot mind my wheel
Psalm 22: Why have You forsaken me?
The Chimney Sweeper
NAYLOR, B.
Dreams of the Sea
PAPINEAU-COUTURE, J.
Quatrains (1947), complete
RIDOUT, G.
Cantiones Mysticae
Choose ANY ONE
SCHAFER, M.
Kinderlieder
Choose ANY TWO
SOMERS, H.
Evocations
Choose ANY ONE
Five Songs for Dark Voice (1956)
Choose ANY TWO
VIVIER, C.
Hymmen an die Nacht (1975)

ASSOCIATE
Pipe Organ (Performer)

Length of Examination: 75 minutes

Examination Fee: Please consult the current examination application form for the schedule of fees.

Co-requisites: Successful completion of THREE written examinations is required for the
                          awarding of the Associate (Performer) Diploma, as follows:
                          Theory 7(A),   Theory(7B),   History 7

Marking

Section	Requirement	Total Mark Possible	Minimum Mark Required
A	SIX LIST PIECES		
	ONE piece from each of		
	List A (Bach Trio)	17	11
	List B (Baroque)	17	11
	List C (Classical/Romantic)	17	11
	List D (20th century, not Canadian)	17	11
	List E (Canadian composition)	17	11
	ONE piece chosen from ANY List	15	10

B	KEYBOARD SKILLS	Pass/Fail	Pass
	Harmonization		
	Transposition		
	Open Score		
	SIGHT READING	Pass/Fail	Pass
	Rhythm Pattern		
	Piano Passage		
	AURAL TESTS	Pass/Fail	Pass

C	OVER-ALL TOTAL	100%	70%

Candidates must obtain:

a) A minimum mark in **each** of the List pieces as specified under Section A.

b) A "Pass" in each section of the Technical Tests & Musicianship Skills as listed under Section B. A candidate will be exempt from these tests in any section(s) in which he/she received the minimum mark in the Grade 10 Conservatory Canada examination. (See under Regulation IV. 7 given above.)

c) A minimum over-all average mark of 70%.

Candidates who fail to obtain the minimum grade in one or more of the requirements listed above (under a, b, or c) shall be required to repeat the ENTIRE EXAMINATION at a subsequent session.

REQUIREMENTS

A) Pieces

Candidates must be prepared to play SIX pieces, at least one of which must be a Prelude/Fantasia/Toccata & Fugue, chosen as follows:

ONE from List A   (Either a Bach Trio Sonata (ANY TWO contrasting movements) or ANY TWO Baroque trio Choral Preludes)

ONE from List B   (Baroque)

ONE from List C   (Classical/Romantic)

ONE from List D   (20th century, not Canadian)

ONE from List F   (Canadian Composition)

ONE chosen from ANY of the above Lists

Pieces should be chosen to contrast in style, key, tempo, mood, etc.. Your choice must include SIX different composers and must also include at least one Prelude/Toccata/Fantasia & Fugue. Memorization is NOT required.

Pieces may be chosen from the Lists or candidates may choose their own repertoire from pieces not included in this Syllabus but of equal difficulty to those given in the Lists. Pieces that appear in Lists for previous Grades *(Organ Syllabus, 1999 edition)* may not be used. Candidates are reminded that own-choice pieces are classified as *Irregular List Pieces* and must be submitted to the Office of the Registrar for approval in accordance with Regulation IV.4 given above.

B) Technical & Musicianship Tests

All technical tests must be played from memory, evenly, with good tone, and logical fingering. Metronome markings should be regarded as *minimum* speeds.

Keyboard Skills

Open Score	*Harmonization*	*Transposition*
To play at sight a vocal score: No C-clefs Manuals only or manuals and pedal, at the candidate's choice. No crossing of parts	To harmonize at simple melody at sight, ending with a Perfect or Plagal cadence, as appropriate. With pedals. Chords - I, IV, and V, root AND 1st inversion. (ii and vi chords may be used but are not required.) Keys - Up to and including four sharps or flatsr No indication of chord changes will be given V7 chords may be used but are not required. Moving bass and passing notes required.	To transpose a simple two-voice passage at sight. Pedal is not required. Up or down a tone or semitone Treble and bass clefs To or from any key with no more than 4 sharps or flats Major AND minor Difficulty: about Grade 3 level.

41

Example: Harmonization

Sight Reading

Candidates are required to perform at sight a) a rhythmic exercise and b) a passage of organ score as described below. The candidate will be given a brief period to scan the score, but not to "practise silently" before beginning to play. Candidates must perform each section without counting aloud. It is recommended that candidates maintain a steady beat, and avoid the unnecessary repetition caused by attempting to correct errors during the performance.

Rhythm	*Organ Passage*
To tap, clap or play on one note (at the candidate's choice) a rhythm in simple or compound time. May include syncopated rhythms, changing-meters, irregular meters, and complex patterns. Length 4-8 bars Time signature any simple or compound time Note values variety of values including ties Rest values variety of values	To play at sight a short piece, with pedals, equal in difficulty to pieces of Grade 6-7 level, in any style or period. May include modulations, changing meters and irregular meters Keys Major & Minor ALL keys Length 16-32 bars

Example: a) Rhythm

Aural Tests

The candidate will be required:

i)   at the candidate's choice, to play back OR sing back to any vowel, the **lower** part of a two-part phrase in a major key, after the Examiner has:

         ✓named the key [up to and including three sharps or flats]
         ✓played the 4-note chord on the tonic in solid form
         ✓played the passage twice.

The parts may begin on ANY note of the tonic chord. Following is the approximate level of difficulty:

ii)   to identify any of the following intervals after the Examiner has played each one once. Intervals may be played in melodic (broken) form OR harmonic (solid) form.

ORGAN (Performer)

ABOVE a note	**BELOW a note**
major and minor 2nd	*major and minor 2nd*
major and minor 3rd	*major and minor 3rd*
perfect 4th	*perfect 4th*
augmented 4th (diminished 5th)	*augmented 4th (diminished 5th)*
perfect 5th	*perfect 5th*
major and minor 6th	*major and minor 6th*
major and minor 7th	*major and minor 7th*
perfect octave	*perfect octave*

iii) to identify any of the following 4-note chords after each has been played once by the Examiner.
major and *minor* chords: root position and first or second inversion [to be played in solid form, close position]
dominant 7th chords: root position or any inversion [to be played in solid form, close position]
diminished 7th chords: root position only [to be played in solid form, open (SATB) position]

iv) to state whether a short piece in *chorale* style is in a *major* or a *minor* key, and whether the final cadence and all internal cadences are **Perfect** (V-I), **Imperfect** (I-V, II-V, IV-V), **Plagal** (IV-I), or **Interrupted/Deceptive** (V-VI). The Examiner will play the passage TWICE; the first time straight through without interruption, the second time stopping at cadence points for the candidate to identify them.

> NOTE: The Associate (Teacher) Diploma is NOT offered in Organ.

Associate Organ List Pieces

LIST A
Baroque Trio

BACH, J.S.
　Trio Sonatas
　　Choose any two movements (fast/slow) from ANY ONE of
　　　BWV 526, 527, 529, 530
　"Eighteen" Chorale Preludes
　　Choose ANY ONE of
　　　Herr Jesu Christ, dich zu uns wend', BWV 655
　　　Nun komm', der Heiden Heiland, BWV 660
　　　Allein Gott in der Höh sei Ehr', BWV 664
　Clavierübung III Chorale Preludes
　　Choose ANY ONE of
　　　BWV 676, 678, 682, 684, 688
　"Schubler" Chorale Preludes
　　Choose ANY ONE of
　　　Ach bleib bei uns, Herr Jesu Christ, BWV 649

LIST A
Baroque

BACH, J.S.
　Prelude & Fugues
　　Choose ANY ONE (complete) of
　　　BWV, 532, 541, 542, 543, 544, 547, 548
　　Prelude & Fugue in E^b, BWV 552
　　　Choose EITHER Prelude OR Fugue
　　Toccata & Fugue in D minor (Dorian), BWV 538
　　Toccata & Fugue in F, BWV 540
　　　Choose EITHER Toccata OR Fugue
　　Toccata, Adagio & Fugue in C, BWV 564
BACH, J.S./VIVALDI
　Concerto No. 2 in A minor, BWV 593 (complete)
BOEHM, G.
　Variations *Freu dich sehr, O meine Seele*
BRUHNS, N.
　Prelude & Fugue in G (le Grand)
　Prelude & Fugue in E minor

BUXTEHUDE, D.
　Chorale Fantasia *Nun freut euch*
　Magnificat primi toni
　Prelude & Fugue in F$^\#$ minor
　Prelude & Fugue in G minor
FRESCOBALDI, G.
　Partita II, sopra l'aria di Monicha
GRIGNY, N. de
　Verbum Supernum (complete)
　Veni Creator (complete)
KREBS, J.L.
　Toccata & Fugue in E
PACHELBEL, J.
　Prelude, Fugue & Ciaconne in D minor
TUNDER, F.
　Chorale Fantasia *Komm, heiliger Geist*

LIST C
Classical/Romantic

BOSSI, E.
　Concert piece in C minor, Op. 130
BRAHMS, J.
　Prelude & Fugue in G minor
　Prelude & Fugue in A minor
ELGAR, E.
　Sonata in G major, Op. 28 (complete)
FRANCK, C.
　Fantasia in A major
　Final, Op. 21
　Prière, Op. 20

　Three Chorals
　　Choose ANY ONE
GIGOUT, E.
　Toccata
GUILMANT, A.
　Sonatas
　　Choose ANY ONE (complete) of
　　　Nos. 1, 2, 3, 4, 6, 8
　Legende et Final Symphonique
HOLLINS, A.
　Concert Overture in C

ORGAN (Repertoire)

LISZT, F.
Prelude & Fugue on B-A-C-H
MENDELSSOHN, F.
Sonatas, Op. 65
Choose ANY ONE (complete) of
Nos. 1, 4, 6
MOZART, W.A.
Fantasy in F minor, K. 608
Adagio in F minor, K. 594
MULET, H.
Tu es petra
REGER, M.
Toccata & Fugue, Op. 59, Nos. 5, 6
Fantasy & Fugue in D minor, Op. 135b
Fantasy on *Ein feste Burg*, Op. 27
REUBKE, J.
Sonata on Psalm 94 (Allegro only)

RHEINBERGER, J.
Sonatas
Choose ANY ONE (complete) of
Nos. 2, 4, 9, 11, 12
SCHUMANN, R.
Six Fugues on B-A-C-H, Op. 60
Choose ANY ONE of
Nos. 2, 5, 6
THUILLE, L.
Sonata in A minor
WIDOR, C.M.
Symphony Op. 42, No. 1
(First *OR* Last movement)
Symphony, Op. 70
(Movements 3 *AND* 4)
Symphony, Op. 71
(Movements 3 *AND* 4)

LIST E
Twentieth Century: not Canadian

AHRENS, J.
Toccata eroica
ALAIN, J.
Intermezzo
Litanies *(Tois Pieces)*
Suite: Scherzo
Trois Danses
Choose ANY ONE
ALBRIGHT, W.
Organbook 1 (complete)
Organbook 2 (movement 1 or 2)
Organbook 3 (Vol. II, Nos. 4,5 &6)
1732: In memoriam Johannes Albrecht
Sweet Sixteenths
ANDRIESSEN, H.
Toccata (1971)
BONNET, J.
Variations de Concert, Op. 1
BORNEFELD, H.
Sonata
Hommage to Chopin
Choose ANY THREE
CAMILIERI, C.
Invocation to the Creator
DEMESSIEUX, J.
Six Studies
Choose ANY ONE
Te Deum, Op. 11
Triptyque (Prelude, Adagio, Fugue)
DISTLER, H.
Orgelsonate, Op. 18 No. 2
Partita on *Wachet Auf*
DUPRÉ, M.
Preludes and Fugues Op. 7
Choose ANY ONE of
Nos. 1, 2, 3
DURUFLÉ, M.
Prélude et Choral Varié *Veni Créator*
Prélude et Fugue sur le nom d'Alain
Suite, Op. 5
Choose EITHER Prélude OR Toccata

GENZMER, H.
Sonata
HINDEMITH, P.
Sonatas
Choose ANY ONE (complete) of
Nos. 1, 2
LANGLAIS, J.
Hymn d'Actions de graces, Op. 5
No. 3
Poèmes Evangeliques
Les Rameaux
Neuf Pièces
Choose ANY ONE of
Chant d'Heroique
Chant de joie
Rhapsodie Gregorienne
Suite Brève
EITHER movements 1 *AND* 2,
OR movements 3 *AND* 4)
Suite Medieval (complete)
Troisième Symphonie
HODDINOTT, A.
Toccata alla Giga
HOWELLS, H.
Six pieces for Organ
Choose ANY ONE of
Nos. 2, 6
LITAIZE, G.
Prélude et Danse Fuguée
LEIGHTON, K.
Prelude, Scherzo and Passacaglia
MESSIAEN, O.
L'Ascension
III. Transport de Joie
La Nativité du Seigneur
IX. Dieu parmi nous
Les corps glorieux
V. La combat de la mort et de la vie
Messe de la Pentecote
V. Sortie

Meditations sur le Mystère
Choose ANY ONE of
Nos. II, V, VI, VII, IX
Livre d'Orgue
Chants d'oiseaux
MILOS SOKOLA
Passacaglia quasi Toccata on B-A-C-H
MULET, H.
Tu es petra *(Esquisses Byzantines)*
NEAR, G.
Roulade
A Triptych of Fugues
PEETERS, F.
Passacaglia & Fugue
Toccata, Fugue et Hymne sur Ave Maris Stella, Op. 28
Variations on an original theme, Op. 58
Variations and Finale, Op. 20
PERSICHETTI, V.
Sonata for Organ, Op. 86
ROREM, N.
A Quaker Reader
Choose ANY ONE of
Nos. 2,5,9, 11
SCHROEDER, H.
Sonata

SOWERBY, L.
Prelude on *The King's Majesty*
Pageant
TOURNEMIRE, C.
Cinq improvisations
Choose ANY ONE of
Petite rhapsodie
Victimae paschali
Ave maris Stella
VIERNE, L.
Pièces de Fantaisie
Choose ANY ONE of
Op. 51: Prélude
Op. 53: Toccata *AND* Feux Follets
Op. 54: Carillon de Westminster *AND* Impromptu
Op. 55: Naiades
Symphony No. 1
Final
Symphony No. 2 (1st mov't - Allegro)
Symphony No. 3 (5th mov't - Final)
Symphony No. 4 (5th mov't - Final)
Symphony No. 5
EITHER 1st mov't OR 5th mov't
Symphony No. 6
EITHER 1st mov't OR 5th mov't

LIST F
Canadian Composition

BALES, G.
Sonatine for Organ (complete)
Toccata
BÉDARD, D.
Rhapsodie sur le nom de Lavoie
BURGE, J.
Dance *(Toronto Organ Series)*
CABENA, B.
Sonata giogoso
CRAWFORD, T.J.
Toccata in F *(Canadian Musical Heritage)*
HEALEY, D.
Organ Sonata No. 2 (complete)
Voluntary No. 3, Op. 1c
HETU, J.
Variations pour Orgue

HOLMAN, D..
Postlude on a Melody by Melchior Vulpius
(Toronto Organ Series)
KRAPF, G.
Partita on "Was Gott tut, das ist wohlgetan"
Totentanz-Prelude & Fugue on a 17th-century Folksong
MATTON, R.
Suite de Pâques
REED, W.
No. 2, Grand Choeur *(Canadian Musical Heritage)*
Concert Overture in C *(Canadian Musical Heritage)*
WATSON HENDERSON. R.
Chromatic Partita
WILLAN, H.
Introduction, Passacaglia & Fugue
Passacaglia No. 2, E minor
WUENSCH, G.
Introduction, Passacaglia & Fugue

ASSOCIATE
Guitar (Performer)

Length of Examination: 75 minutes

Examination Fee: Please consult the current examination application form for the schedule of fees.

Co-requisites: Successful completion of THREE written examinations is required for the awarding of
                           the Associate (Performer) Diploma, as follows:
                           Theory 7(A),   Theory(7B),   History 7

Marking

Section	Requirement	Total Mark Possible	Minimum Mark Required
A	FIVE LIST PIECES		
	To be performed from memory		
	ONE from List A (Baroque Suite)	26	17
	ONE from List B (Sonata)	26	17
	TWO from List C (20th Century)	16	10
		16	10
	ONE Piece of your OWN Choice (Any period)	16	10

Section	Requirement	Total Mark Possible	Minimum Mark Required
B	TECHNICAL TESTS	Pass/Fail	Pass
	Scales		
	Arpeggios		
	Harmonization		
	SIGHT READING	Pass/Fail	Pass
	Rhythm Pattern		
	Guitar Passage		
	AURAL TESTS	Pass/Fail	Pass

Section	Requirement	Total Mark Possible	Minimum Mark Required
C	OVER-ALL TOTAL	100%	70%

Candidates must obtain:

   a) A minimum mark in **each** of the List pieces as specified under Section A.

   b) A "Pass" in each section of the Technical Tests & Musicianship Skills as listed under Section B.
A candidate will be exempt from these tests in any section(s) he/she received the minimum mark in the
Grade 10 Conservatory Canada examination. (See Regulation IV. 7 given above.)

   c) A minimum over-all average mark of 70%

*Candidates who fail to obtain the minimum grade in one or more of the requirements listed above (under
a, b, or c) shall be required to repeat the ENTIRE EXAMINATION at a subsequent session.*

REQUIREMENTS

A) Pieces

Candidates must be prepared to play FIVE pieces chosen as follows:

ONE from List A (complete sonata)

ONE from List B (complete suite)

TWO from List C (20th century)

ONE additional pieces of your own choice, approximately of equal difficulty to those pieces in the Lists. May be in any style or period. Prior approval is NOT required.

Pieces should be chosen to contrast in style, key, tempo, mood, etc.. Your pieces must include FIVE different composers All pieces must be performed from memory.

Pieces for *Lists A, B, and C*, may be chosen from the Lists given or candidates may choose their own repertoire from pieces not included in this Syllabus but of equal difficulty to those given in the Lists. Pieces that appear in Lists for previous Grades *(Piano Syllabus, 1999 edition)* may not be used. Candidates are reminded that own-choice pieces substituted for Lists A, B, and C are classified as *Irregular List Pieces* and must be submitted to the Office of the Registrar for approval in accordance with Regulation IV.4 given above.

Technical Tests

Conservatory Canada's booklet *Guitar Technique Book* (1999) contains notational examples for all technical requirements.

All technical tests must be played from memory, evenly, with good tone, logical fingering. Metronome markings should be regarded as *minimum* speeds. The number of octaves are as given in *Guitar Technique Book* (1999).

KEYS REQUIRED IN GRADE TEN

	Keys
Major	ALL Keys
Minor	ALL Keys

SCALES

To be played from memory, ascending AND descending, in the keys stated.

Scale fingerings: Right hand, fingered i-m, m-a, and i-a (to be specified by the examiner), using rest and free stroke. Use only movable, closed string left-hand fingering (except open 6th string).

	Keys	M.M. $\quad \downarrow =$	Articulation
Major	All keys	112 112	in sixteenth notes AND in triplet eighth notes
Minor (Harmonic AND Melodic)	All keys	112 112	in sixteenth notes AND in triplet eighth notes

GUITAR (Performer)

Repeated	All keys	84	in quintuplet sixteenth notes AND in sextuplet sixteenth notes
Slur	G, A	144	in compound triplet eighth notes
3rd & 6th	A	104	solid in eighth notes AND broken in sixteenth notes
Chromatic	beginning on E	112 112	in sixteenth notes AND in triplet eighth notes

Note: Do NOT repeat the upper tonic note.
Do NOT play either the tonic chord or a cadence at the end of the scale.

ARPEGGIOS
To be played ascending AND descending in the keys stated.

	Keys	Position	M.M. $\bullet$ =	Note Values
Major	All keys		104	in eighth notes
Minor	All keys		104	in eighth notes
Dominant 7th	of All Major keys		104	in eighth notes
Diminished 7th	of All minor keys		104	in eighth notes

HARMONIZATION
Candidates are required to harmonize a simple melody at sight. Candidates are expected to play both the melody AND an appropriate accompaniment in at least a two-voice texture. Use of unessential tones in the accompaniment is encouraged but not required. No indication of chord of chord changes will be given.

Keys of   A, E, F Major
          f#,d, Minor
Chords   I, i, IV, iv, V or V^7 (root and first inversion)
          ii and vi chords may be used but are not required.

Example

Sight Reading
Candidates are required to perform at sight a) a rhythmic exercise and b) a passage of guitar score as described below. The candidate will be given a brief period to scan the score, but not to "practise silently" before beginning to

play. Candidates must perform each section without counting aloud. It is recommended that candidates maintain a steady beat, and avoid the unnecessary repetition caused by attempting to correct errors during the performance.

Rhythm	*Guitar Passage*
To tap, clap or play on one note (at the candidate's choice) a rhythm in simple or compound time. May include syncopated rhythms, changing-meters, irregular meters, and complex patterns.	To play at sight a short guitar piece equal in difficulty to pieces of Grade 6-7 level, in any style or period. May include modulations, changing meters and irregular meters
Length 4-8 bars Time signature any simple or compound time Note values variety of values including ties Rest values variety of values	Keys Major & Minor ALL keys Length 16-32 bars

Example: a) Rhythm

Aural Tests

The candidate will be required:

i) at the candidate's choice, to play back OR sing back to any vowel, the **lower** part of a two-part phrase in a major key, after the Examiner has:
    ✓ named the key [up to and including three sharps or flats]
    ✓ played the 4-note chord on the tonic in solid form
    ✓ played the passage twice.

The parts may begin on ANY note of the tonic chord. Following is the approximate level of difficulty:

ii) to identify any of the following intervals after the Examiner has played each one once. Intervals may be played in melodic (broken) form OR harmonic (solid) form.

ABOVE a note
major and minor 2nd
major and minor 3rd
perfect 4th
augmented 4th (diminished 5th)
perfect 5th
major and minor 6th
major and minor 7th
perfect octave

BELOW a note
major and minor 2nd
major and minor 3rd
perfect 4th
augmented 4th (diminished 5th)
perfect 5th
major and minor 6th
major and minor 7th
perfect octave

iii) to identify any of the following 4-note chords after each has been played once by the Examiner.

major and *minor* chords: root position and first or second inversion [to be played in solid form, close position]

dominant 7th chords: root position or any inversion [to be played in solid form, close position]

diminished 7th chords: root position only [to be played in solid form, open (SATB) position]

iv) to state whether a short piece in *chorale* style is in a *major* or a *minor* key, and whether the final cadence and all internal cadences are **Perfect** (V-I), **Imperfect** (I-V, II-V, IV-V), **Plagal** (IV-I), or **Interrupted/Deceptive** (V-VI). The Examiner will play the passage TWICE; the first time straight through without interruption, the second time stopping at cadence points for the candidate to identify them.

| NOTE: The Associate (Teacher) Diploma is NOT offered in Guitar |

Associate Guitar List Pieces

LIST A
Complete Suite

BACH, J.S.
Choose ANY Suite (complete) for Lute or Cello that does not
appear in the Lists for previous grades.

WEISS, S.L.
Intavolatura di liuto, I
Choose ANY ONE of
Suite No. 3 (complete)
Suite No. 8 (complete)
Suite No. 14 (complete)
Partita in A minor

LIST B
Complete Sonata

Choose ANY ONE Sonata (complete) that does not appear in
any Lists for previous grades by ANY ONE of the following
composers

GUILIANI, M.
PONCE, M.
SOR, F.

LIST C
(20th Century)

ARNOLD, M./BREAM	
Fantasy for Guitar	Faber
BREAU, L.	
Freight Train	Mel Bay
BROUWER, L.	
Tarantos	Eschig
BENNET, R.R.	
Impromptus	Universal
Choose ANY TWO of	
Nos. 5, 6, 7, 8, 9, 10	
BRITTEN, B.	
Nocturnal	Faber
CARTER, E.	
Changes	Boosey
DODGSON, S.	
Partita (complete)	Doberman
DUARTE, J.W.	
In Honorem Ioanni Doulandi, Op. 97	NovaScribe
GIBSON, G.	
Cantilena	NovaScribe
HENZE, H.W.	
Royal Winter Music	Guitar Arc.
Choose ANY ONE of	
Sonata No. 1 (complete)	
Sonata No. 2 (complete)	
SCHAFER, R.M.	
Le Cri de Merlin	CMC
TAKEMITSU, T.	
Folios (complete)	Sal

THEORY 7(A)

HARMONY & COUNTERPOINT
(Associate Diploma)

ONE PAPER: **Time: 3 Hours**

RECOMMENDED TEXTS   *No one text is complete insofar as these requirements are concerned and, though discrepancies between sources are not unusual, candidates are encouraged to consult a variety of sources. A selective list of theory resource books may be found under the Bibliography section at the end of the Theory & History Syllabus (1999 edition). However, though candidates may choose any text book(s), the following are recommended.*

Gauldin, Robert, *Harmonic Practice in Tonal Music*
(Norton, 1997)
Workbook and CD recording of musical examples available

Trythall, H. Gilbert, *Eighteenth-Century Counterpoint*
(Brown & Benchmark, 1993)

CO-REQUISITE   Successful completion of Theory 7(A) is required to obtain the ASSOCIATE DIPLOMA.

Note: Musical terminology as used in either of the recommended texts is acceptable for examination purposes.

REQUIREMENTS
Candidates must know all requirements for all grades up to and including Theory 6, AND additional requirements as follows

Keys required for this examination

Major	ALL Keys
Minor	ALL Keys

Candidates are expected to be familiar with the use of the following

Major, Minor, Augmented, Diminished Chords (root position and inversions)
Advanced use of Secondary (Applied) Dominant chords (root position and inversions)
Advanced use of Secondary (Applied) Diminished 7th chords (root position and inversions)

Altered Chords
    Neapolitan 6th chord
    Augmented 6th chords

All Non-chord Tones
Modulation to any key

1. Harmony (Chorale Style)	
	Harmonize for SATB in chorale style, a melody and/or bass (figured or unfigured), observing the accepted rules of voice leading, and using ●Modulation to any key ●Neapolitan chords ●Augmented 6th chords ●Suspensions, and non-harmonic notes ●The question will provide a portion already completed to indicate style and period (i.e. Baroque, Classical or Romantic) ●Harmonic analysis may be required

2. Harmony (Keyboard Style)	
	Continue a keyboard accompaniment for a given solo line (for either voice or instrument) for approximately 8-12 bars in a similar style. The opening portion of the accompaniment will be given to indicate the style. The answer should include ●Modulation to any key and return to the tonic ●A rhythm and harmony of musical interest, flow, and unity ●Harmonic analysis may be required

3. Counterpoint	
	The candidate may choose **EITHER** To extend a given opening to create a two-part contrapuntal composition of 16 -20 bars in length in the style of a Baroque Invention. ●Include points of imitation and show motivic unity ●Include modulations consistent with the period ●Give chordal analysis of implied harmony **OR** TWO fugal subjects will be given. The candidate will provide an Answer (real or tonal) for each subject. The candidate will then provide a countersubject in invertible counterpoint for either ONE of the subjects. ●Include a modulatory link (or bridge) between the subject and answer, if necessary ●Give chordal analysis of implied harmony

NOTE: A study of the following works (any edition) will assist candidates in preparing for the examination:

        Bach, J.S.   *Two-Part Inventions*
        Bach, J.S.   *Well-Tempered Clavier, Vols. I and II*
        Bach, J.S.   *The Art of Fugue*
        Riemenschneider, A. (ed.) *371 Harmonized Chorales* (Schirmer)

and also a selection of
        Lieder representing Schubert, Schumann, Brahms, and Wolf

THEORY 7(B)

FORM & ANALYSIS
(Associate Diploma)

ONE PAPER: **Time: 3 Hours**

RECOMMENDED TEXTS   *No one text is complete insofar as these requirements are concerned and, though discrepancies between sources are not unusual, candidates are encouraged to consult a variety of sources. A selective list of theory resource books may be found under the Bibliography section at the end of the Theory & History Syllabus (1999 edition). However, though candidates may choose any text book(s), the following are recommended.*

Berry, Wallace, *Form in Music* (Prentice Hall, 1986)

CO-REQUISITE   Successful completion of Theory 7(B) is required to obtain the ASSOCIATE DIPLOMA

Note: *Musical terminology as used in the recommended text is acceptable for examination purposes.*

REQUIREMENTS
It is recommended that candidates complete Theory 7(A) before proceeding to Theory 7(B).

Keys required for this examination

Major	ALL Keys
Minor	ALL Keys

1. Formal Structures	Be familiar with the formal characteristics and historical development of the following forms: ●Binary (all types) ●Ternary ●Rondo ●Theme and Variations (including Chaconne & Passacaglia) ●Sonata Form ●Fugue ●Song types (such as strophic, modified-strophic, through-composed, etc.)

2. Analysis	Provide detailed analysis for given musical examples, representing no more that THREE of the above forms, as follows: ●Identify key ●Trace thematic and motivic development ●Mark phrases and cadences ●Identify main key centres, points of modulation, key relationships and structural divisions ●Harmonic analysis (as requested for selected passages) using chord symbols and figures. Non-harmonic notes to be circled and labelled

HISTORY 7

ONE PAPER   **Time: 3 Hours**

RECOMMENDED TEXTS   See Recommended texts listed below

PRE-REQUISITES   Candidates must complete both History 5 and History 6 (in any order) before proceeding to History 7

CO-REQUISITE   Successful completion of History 7 is required to obtain the ASSOCIATE DIPLOMA

Requirements

The course is divided into two parts as follows:

Part I   Submission of a brief essay (minimum of 2,000 words)
Part II   A written examination

PART I: Essay on Canadian Music

Candidates will prepare a brief essay on ANY ONE of the topics listed below, to be enclosed at the time of the examination with the completed examination paper (Part II). Because this course is a diploma level course, it is assumed that candidates are able to accumulate and organize information on their chosen topic from a number of different sources, and to express themselves clearly in writing. Candidates may use whatever resource material, both in print and on recording, they feel is important. All sources should be properly documented, with footnotes as appropriate and a bibliography.

The essay is to be typewritten on plain white paper, double-spaced, with margins of at least 1 inch. The cover page should include only the candidate's examination number and the title of the essay.

Essays submitted previously to other institutions, for credit or otherwise, may NOT be submitted for this examination.

Essay Topics:

Healey Willan and his influence on the next generation of composers in Canada

The composition of choral music in Canada since 1945

Three leading composers of music for piano in Canada since 1945
[Three composers to be chosen by the candidate]

The foundation for new directions in Canadian music for the 21st century
[Discuss the works and influence of ANY TWO composers active in the 1990s]

Film music by Canadians

The use of indigenous native music in Canadian compositions.

R. Murray Schafer: An experimenter

Violet Archer, Jean Coulthard and Barbara Pentland: Ahead of their time?

The stage works of Harry Somers

Candidates may also submit their own choice of topic to the Registrar for approval. Requests must be made in writing and be received at the Conservatory office at least 30 days before the deadline for application for the examination sesssion.

PART II: Written Examination

Candidates will choose to complete a detailed study of ANY ONE of the following historical periods:

A)	***Renaissance & Baroque***	
	Recommended Texts	Brown, Howard Mayer: *Music in the Renaissance* (Prentice Hall, 1976)
		Palisca, Claude M.: *Baroque Music* (Prentice Hall, 1991)
B)	***Classical***	
	Recommended Text	Downs, Philip G.: *Classical Music: The Era of Haydn, Mozart and Beethoven* (Norton, 1991)
C)	***Romantic & Impressionism***	
	Recommended Text	Rosen, Charles: *The Romantic Generation* (Harvard University Press, 1995)
D)	***20th-Century***	
	Recommended Text	Machlis, Joseph: *An Introduction to Contemporary Music* (Norton, 1979)
E)	***Canadian Music***	
	Recommended Text	McGee, Timothy: *The Music of Canada* (Norton, 1985)

Candidates should concentrate on historical chronology, leading composers and their influence, musical examples, and the development of styles, forms and compositional techniques. *Candidates are expected to support their answers with appropriate musical examples.* Choose ANY FOUR works (each differing in composer and genre) that you consider representative of the period you are studying and through the study of scores and recordings, be prepared to discuss and refer to them in the written examination.

The selective list of reference and text books given in the Bibliography section at the end of this Syllabus will provide additional sources of information that candidates will find helpful.

Examination Paper

All questions will be based on information contained in standard written sources for the period chosen, and also on musical scores and recordings of typical examples.

The format of the question paper will be as follows:

Type of Questions	Total Marks
PART II (Examination Paper) General questions requiring short answer of three or four lines in paragraph form. Some choice will be given.	30
1 essay-type question on the chosen works	25
1 general essay-type question on the period	25
TOTAL MARKS FOR PART II (EXAMINATION PAPER)	**80**
TOTAL MARKS FOR PART I (ESSAY)	**20**

PEDAGOGY 7

ONE WRITTEN PAPER   **Time: 3 Hours**

RECOMMENDED TEXTS   None. Contact the Conservatory for a suggested Reading List.

PRE-REQUISITES   None. Though it is highly recommended that candidates complete Theory 6, History 5 and 6, and reach a performance standard of Grade 10 Practical before undertaking Pedagogy 7.

NOTE   The Written Pedagogy Examination is offered only in *Piano, Voice, Violin*

Requirements (For All Instruments)

Candidates must be prepared to answer questions on the following topics:

   i) Pedagogical principles involved in
        teaching the first lesson to both young and mature beginners
        the teacher-student relationship
        introducing new repertoire, technique, and musical concepts
        teaching musicianship skills (including aural training, sight reading, memorizing, practice methods)
        developing goals and materials grade by grade

   ii) Comparative evaluation of beginner Method books

   iii) Mechanism and function of the instrument.

   iv) Performance style, interpretation, ornamentation, and form

   v)   Goals and materials (including studies, repertoire, technique)

   vi) Detection and correction of common problems

Candidates should be familiar with the appropriate viva voce requirements of the Practical (Teachers) requirements.

Piano and Voice candidates will be required to demonstrate a knowledge of the repertoire in Conservatory Canada's *New Millennium Series*.

Examination Paper

All questions will require answers in essay form. Candidates will be expected to support their answers with musical titles. composers and examples, as appropriate. Some evaluation and grading of selected pieces may be required.

LICENTIATE
(All Instruments & Voice)

Length of Examination: 75 minutes

Examination Fee: Please consult the current examination application form for the schedule of fees.

Pre-requisite: Successful completion of the Associate Diploma in Music from Conservatory Canada or The Western Board or Western Ontario Conservatory of Music

IMPORTANT NOTE: *Licentiate examinations are offered only in London, Edmonton and other major centres to be determined from time to time. Please consult the Conservatory for the Licentiate examination centre nearest you.*

A panel of TWO examiners will conduct the examination.

Marking

Section	Requirement	Total Mark Possible
A	RECITAL To be performed from memory (except organ) Musicianship & Presentation Accuracy Choice of Repertoire	 45 40 5

B	PROGRAM NOTES	10

C	OVER-ALL TOTAL	100%

In order to be awarded the Licentiate Diploma, candidates must obtain a minimum over-all mark of 70%.

Candidates who fail to obtain the minimum grade will be required to repeat the ENTIRE EXAMINATION at a subsequent session.

REQUIREMENTS

A) Pieces

Candidates must perform a full-length recital consisting of approximately 50-60 minutes of music. The Conservatory will schedule the recital to take place in an examination session and the recital may be open to the public at no charge. The Conservatory will provide printed programs. There will be a 15-minute intermission. Candidates must provide their own piano accompanist if one is required.

There are no List Pieces. The choice of repertoire is entirely at the discretion of the candidate, and must be chosen and arranged to form an artistically well-balanced recital program, varied in style and period. In choosing your examination recital repertoire, the following will apply:

i) All candidates must include at least one work by a Canadian composer.

ii) Instrumentalists must include at least one complete sonata. Guitarists may substitute a complete suite. Singers must include at least one complete song cycle.

iii) One piece may include the use of obbligato instrument(s). The candidate will be responsible for all arrangements with the obbligato player.

iv) Instrumentalists may include a concerto (complete). Piano and Guitar candidates will be responsible for all arrangements with a pianist to play the orchestral part. Piano candidates will also be responsible to ensure that a second piano is available.

v) Licentiate candidates may NOT use pieces included in Conservatory Canada's Syllabus List Pieces (Grades 1-10), or any other piece they performed previously in an Associate practical examination.

The complete program requires the prior approval of the Conservatory. Candidates must submit their proposed program, in writing, to the Office of the Registrar at least 90 days before the scheduled date of the recital. Candidates are advised to obtain this approval as early as possible because the Conservatory cannot be responsible for inappropriate choices of repertoire.

B) Program Notes

After the program has been approved, candidates must prepare TWO sets of written program notes on the pieces to be performed.

i) One set of comprehensive notes, giving information about the historical and musical significance of each piece, and commenting upon its musical features and form.

ii) A concise, condensed version of the comprehensive notes, suitable for the general public, and appropriately edited for inclusion in the printed program.

Each set of program notes must be typewritten, and double-spaced, and must be submitted to the Office of the Registrar at least 30 days before the scheduled date of the recital.

BIBLIOGRAPHY

The following books are useful for study reference or teaching purposes.

DICTIONARIES AND ENCYCLOPEDIAS

Baker's Biographical Dictionary of Musicians	N. Slonimsky, ed. (Schirmer, 1984)
Encyclopedia of Music in Canada	H. Kallmann, G. Potvin & K. Winters, eds. (University of Toronto Press, 1992)
New Harvard Dictionary of Music	D.M. Randel, ed. (Harvard University Press, 1986)
Oxford Companion to Music	P. Scholes, ed. (Oxford University Press, 1984)
The Concise Oxford Dictionary of Opera	H. Rosenthal & J.H. Warrack, eds. (Oxford University Press, 1992)
The New Grove Dictionary of Jazz	B. Kernfeld, ed. (MacMillan, 1988)
The New Grove Dictionary of Music and Musicians	S. Sadie, ed. (Macmillan, 1980)
The New Grove Dictionary of Opera	S. Sadie, ed. (Macmillan, 1992)
The Oxford Companion to Music	D. Arnold, ed., (Oxford University Press, 1983)

ANTHOLOGIES

Bach, J.S.	*371 Harmonized Chorales*, ed. A. Riemenschneider (Schirmer, 1941)
Bach, J.S.	*48 Fugues in Open Score*, ed. W. Andrews (Gordon V. Thompson, 1988)
Burkhart, Charles	*Anthology for Musical Analysis* (Holt, Rinehart & Winston, 1986)
Downs, Philip G.	*Anthology of Classical Music* (Norton, 1992)
Forney, Kristine, ed.	*The Norton Scores: An Anthology for Study* (Norton, 1995)
Hoppin, Richard H.	*Anthology of Medieval Music* (Norton, 1978)
Palisca, Claude V., ed.	*The Norton Anthology of Western Music* (Norton, 1988)

BOOKS

Harmony and Counterpoint

Andrews, William G. & Molly Sclater	*Elements of Eighteenth Century Counterpoint* (Thompson, 1986)
Andrews, William G. & Molly Sclater	*Materials of Western Music, Parts I-III* (Thompson, 1987-88)
Benjamin, Thomas	*Counterpoint in the Style of J.S. Bach* (Schirmer, 1986)
Kennan, Kent W.	*Counterpoint: Based on 18th Century Practice* (Prentice Hall, 1987)
Mason, N.B.	*The Essentials of Eighteenth-Century Counterpoint* (W.C. Brown, 1977)
Milner, Anthony	*Harmony for Class Teaching, Books I and II* (Novello, 1972)
Morris, R.O.	*Introduction to Counterpoint* (Oxford University Press, 1975)
Piston, Walter	*Harmony*, rev. DeVoto (Norton, 1987)
Ottman, Robert W.	*Advanced Harmony* (Prentice-Hall, 1992)

Form and Analysis

Burkhart, Charles.	*Anthology for Musical Analysis* (Holt, Rinehart & Winston, 1986)
Creighton, Arthur.	*A Workbook for Music Analysis* (Waterloo, 1980)
Iliffe, Francis.	*Bach's 48 Preludes and Fugues Analysed for Students*, 2 volumes. (Novello, n.d.)
Lovelock, William	*Form in Brief* (Elkin, 1954)
Macpherson, Stewart.	*Form in Music* (Stainer and Bell, 1978)
Morris, R.O.	*The Structure of Music: An Outline for Students* (Oxford University Press, 1985)
Rosen, Charles.	*Sonata Forms* (Norton, 1988)
Stein, Leon.	*Structure and Style* (Summy-Birchard, 1979)
Tovey, Donald, F.	*A Companion to the Beethoven Pianoforte Sonatas* (AMS Press, 1976)

Music History

General

Abraham, Gerald	*The Concise Oxford History of Music* (Oxford University Press, 1991)
Grout, Donald Jay	*A History of Western Music* (Norton, 1988)
Lang, Paul Henry	*Music in Western Civilization* (Norton, 1941)

BIBLIOGRAPHY

Poultney, David   *Studying Music History* (Prentice Hall, 1983)
Ulrich, Homer & Paul A. Pisk   *A History of Music and Musical Style* (Harcourt Brace Jovanovich, 1963)

Renaissance
Brown, Howard Mayer   *Music in the Renaissance* (Prentice Hall, 1976)
Hoppin, Richard H.   *Medieval Music* (Norton, 1978)
Reese, Gustave, et al.   *The New Grove High Renaissance Masters* (Norton, 1984)
Seay, Albert   *Music in the Medieval World* (Prentice Hall, 1975)
Yudkin, Jeremy   *Music in Medieval Europe* (Prentice Hall, 1989)

Baroque
Anthony, James, et al.   *The New Grove French Baroque Masters* (Norton, 1986)
Arnold, Denis, et al.   *The New Grove Italian Baroque Masters* (Norton, 1984)
Palisca, Claude M.   *Baroque Music* (Prentice Hall, 1991)

Classical
Downs, Philip G.   *Classical Music: The Era of Haydn, Mozart and Beethoven* (Norton, 1992)
Kerman, Joseph & Alan Tyson   *The New Grove Beethoven* (Norton, 1983)
Larsen, Jens P. & Georg Feder   *The New Grove Haydn* (Norton, 1983)
Pauly, Reinhard G.   *Music in the Classical Period* (Prentice Hall, 1988)
Rosen, Charles   *The Classical Style: Haydn, Mozart, Beethoven* (1972)
Rushton, Julian   *Classical Music. A Concise History from Gluck to Beethoven* (Thames, 1986)
Sadie, Stanley   *The New Grove Mozart* (Norton, 1983)

Romantic
Abraham, Gerald, et al.   *The New Grove Russian Masters II* (Norton, 1986)
Brown, David, et al.   *The New Grove Russian Masters I* (Norton, 1986)
Brown, Maurice & Eric Sams   *The New Grove Schubert* (Norton, 1990)
Cooke, Deryck, et al.   *The New Grove Late Romantic Masters* (Norton, 1985)
Deathridge, John & C. Dahlhaus   *The New Grove Wagner* (Norton, 1984)
Longyear, Rey M.   *Nineteenth-Century Romanticism in Music* (Prentice Hall, 1973)
Rosen, Charles   *The Romantic Generation* (Harvard University Press, 1995)
Temperley, Nicholas, et al.   *The New Grove Early Romantic Masters I* (Norton, 1985)
Warrack, John, et al.   *The New Grove Early Romantic Masters II* (Norton, 1985)

Twentieth Century
Antokoletz, Elliott   *Twentieth-Century Music* (Prentice Hall, 1992)
Austin, William W., et al.   *The New Grove Twentieth Century American Masters* (Norton, 1987)
Brindle, Reginald S.   *The New Music: The Avant-Garde Since 1945* (Oxford University Press, 1987)
Griffiths, Paul   *A Concise History of Avant-Garde Music: from Debussy to Boulez* (Oxford , 1978)
Griffiths, Paul   *Modern Music: The Avant-Garde Since 1945* (Dent, 1981)
Lampert, Vera, et al.   *The New Grove Modern Masters* (Norton, 1984)
Machlis, Joseph   *An Introduction to Contemporary Music* (Norton, 1979)
Manning, Peter   *Electronic and Computer Music* (Oxford University Press, 1993)
McVeagh, Diana, et al.   *The New Grove Twentieth Century English Masters* (Norton, 1986)
Nectoux, Jean-Michel, et al.   *The New Grove Twentieth Century French Masters* (Norton, 1986)
Neighbour, Oliver, et al.   *The New Grove Second Viennese School* (Norton, 1983)
Oliver, Paul, et al.   *The New Grove Gospel, Blues and Jazz* (Norton, 1986)
Perle, George   *Serial Composition and Atonality* (University of California Press, 1991)
Simms, Bryan R.   *Music of the Twentieth Century: Style and Structure* (Schirmer, 1986)
Watkins, Glenn   *Soundings: Music of the Twentieth Century* (Schirmer, 1988)

Canadian Music
Kallmann, Helmut   *A History of Music in Canada* (University of Toronto Press, 1992)
McGee, Timothy   *The Music of Canada* (Norton, 1985)
Proctor, George A.   *Canadian Music of the Twentieth Century* (University of *Toronto Press, 1980)

Various Pamphlets on individual Canadian composers produced by Performing Rights Organization of Canada Ltd. and The Canadian Music Centre.

BIBLIOGRAPHY

Pedagogy

Piano

Ahrens & Atkinson	*For All Piano Teachers* (Harris)
Agay, D.	*Teaching Piano, Vols. I and II* (Yorktown)
Bach, C.P.E.	*Essay on the True Art of Keyboard Playing* (Norton)
Bastien, J.W.	*How to Teach the Piano Successfully* (Kjos)
Bolton, H.	*How to Practice* (Novello)
	On Teaching the Piano (H.W. Gray)
Clark, F.	*Questions and Answers: Practical Advice for Piano Teachers* (The Instrumentalist Co.)
Foldes, A.	*Keys to the Keyboard* (Oxford)
Gat, J.	*The Technique of Piano Playing* (Collets)
Gillespie, J.	*Five Centuries of Keyboard Music* (Dover)
Hinson, M.	*Guide to the Pianist's Repertoire* (Indiana Press)
Hutcheson, G.	*The Literature of the Piano* (Knopf)
Last, J.	*Interpretation for the Piano Student* (Oxford)
	The Young Pianist (Oxford)
Magrath, J.	*The Pianist's Guide to Standard Teaching and Performance Literature* (Alfred)
Matthay, T.	*Interpretation of Music* (Oxford)
Newman, W.	*The Pianist's Problems* (Harper)
Rubinstein, B.	*Outlines of Piano Pedagogy* (Fischer)
	Sight Reading and Memorizing (Fischer)
Schonberg, H.	*The Great Pianists*
Uszler, G	*The Well-Tempered Keyboard Teacher* (Schirmer)

Voice

Appleman, D. R.	*The Science of Vocal Pedagogy* (Indiana Univ. Press)
Behnke, E.	*The Mechanism of the Human Voice* (Curwen)
Bernac, P.	*The Interpretation of French Song* (Norton)
Colorni, E.	*Singer's Italian* (Schirmer)
Cristy, V.A.	*Foundations in Singing* (Wm. A. Brown)
Garcia, M.	*A Complete Treatise on the Art of Singing, Parts I & II* (Da Capo)
	Hints on Singing (Patelson)
Grubb, T.	*Singing in French* (Schirmer)
Kagen, S.	*On Studying Singing* (Dover)
Lawson, J.T.	*Full-Throated Ease* (Belwin Mills)
Lehman, L.	*How to Sing* (MacMillan)
	More than Singing (Dover)
Manén, L.	*The Art of Singing* (Faber)
Marshall, M.	*The Singer's Manual of English Diction* (Schirmer)
Martin, G.	*The Opera Companion* (John Murray)
Moore, G.	*Singer and Accompanist* (Greenwood)
Osborne, C.	*The Concert Song Companion* (Da Capo)
Reed, J/	*The Schubert Song Companion* (Faber)
Reid, C.L.	*Bel Canto* (Patelson)
	Voice: Psyche and Soma (Patelson)
	The Free Voice (Patelson)
	A Dictionary of Vocal Terminology (Patelson)
Rose, A.	*The Singer and the Voice* (Faber)
Vennard, W.	*Singing: The Mechanism and Technique* (Carl Fisher)
Fuchs, V.	*The Art of Singing* (Calder & Boyars)

Kobbé's Complete Opera Book, ed. Earl of Harwood (Bodley Head)

NOTES